ORKl

This guide, reprinted through popular demand, provides an excellent insight into the architecture of the Orkney Islands and at the same time introduces the reader to the great depth of physical, social and cultural traditions that have helped to mould the islands' built heritage.

The publication will be of great interest to local people, historians, design and building professionals and tourists, who will find, through the excellent illustrations and descriptions, new areas of interest in the local architecture which can be keenly followed up and explored.

The volume makes a very welcome return to the series of RIAS Illustrated Architectural Guides to Scotland which have become compulsory reading for the interested visitor.

Camuo.

COLIN I MUNRO RIBA FRIAS
President
Inverness Architectural Association

The Rutland Press wishes to thank the following supporters whose assistance secured this reprint : Elf Consortium; Orkney Islands Council; Inverness Architectural Association; The John M Archer Charitable Trust; Stockan, Sloan & Sinclair Macdonald and Orkney Tourist Board.

elf consortium

Elf Exploration · Texaco · LASMO · ARCO · Intrepid

© Leslie Burgher 1991

Series editor: Charles McKean
Series consultant: David Walker
Editorial consultant: Duncan McAra
Cover design: Dorothy Steedman

The Rutland Press ISBN 1 873190 02 6
1st published 1991 Reprinted 1999

Front cover illustrations
Main: Broch of Gurness (Burgher)
Insert: Ring of Brodgar (Burgher)

Back cover illustrations
Top: Earls Palace Kirkwall (Burgher)
Below: St Magnus Cathedral (Burgher)

Origination by Kyte Design & Production
Printed by Inglis Allen

Orkney is made up of a group of more than 70 islands, holms and skerries lying 15km off the northernmost tip of Scotland. The main approach is from the south across the restless waters of the Pentland Firth, a narrow channel through which the waters of the Atlantic Ocean and the North Sea pour back and forth twice daily. The first sight of the islands is of the south-western wall of Hoy whose red sandstone cliffs rise to a dizzying 400m. However, on entering Hoy Sound, it becomes apparent that the scatter of green and brown islands which lie behind it are of a gentler and more fertile form.

Temperatures, thanks to the surrounding sea, are moderate. Prolonged periods of snow or frost are rare, although summers are cool; and it is, for obvious reasons, a damp climate. Wind is almost always present and can be severe. However, the variability of the weather gives an ever-changing play of light across land and water with often brilliant colours and dramatic open skies, unobstructed in this low, treeless landscape.

The climate was even milder more than 5000 years ago when the first settlers built their homes. Orkney appears to have been a Pictish kingdom and was literally at the centre of the Norse world. Equidistant from Stockholm and Reykjavik it became, through the importance of its situation and distance from centres of government, a virtual kingdom, with the Norse Earls of Orkney controlling land as far away as Ireland. In the 18th and 19th centuries the islands became an important base for the pursuit of whales and herring. In this century, two World Wars resulted in the re-emergence of the islands' strategic position in the North Atlantic; in the last decade Orkney has had an important role to play in the development of North Sea oil.

The landscape is, with the exception of the island of Hoy, low and gently rolling: a product of the upraised and lightly faulted basin into which debris from the Caledonian Mountains was washed to form a variety of sedimentary rocks. Laid down in thin flagstone beds, since earliest times these have been readily available as building material or, in thinner forms, roof covering. Stone is abundant and easily worked compensating for a relative shortage of timber on the islands.

As a result, Orkney possesses an unparalleled repertoire of buildings from one of Europe's oldest houses (c.3500BC) to the world's most powerful wind generator (1987) with structures representing all the varied periods between.

Opposite Melsetter, Hoy (photo Leslie Burgher)

Fishing station, Tankerness

How to use this Guide

Orkney has been better served by writers and historians than almost any other area in Scotland. Among these, Edwin Muir's *An Autobiography*, Eric Linklater's *Orkney and Shetland*, and George Mackay Brown's *Orkney Tapestry* and *Portrait of Orkney* are outstanding as literary introductions, while William Thomson's *History of Orkney* and B H Hossack's *Kirkwall in the Orkneys* are essential reading for the scholar of Orkney history. The story of the Vikings in Orkney is best read in Hermann Palsson and Paul Edwards' translation of *Orkneyinga Saga* whilst the Orkney crofters' way of life is best described in John Firth's *Reminiscences of an Orkney Parish* and Alexander Fenton's *The Northern Isles*. This volume, by contrast, is primarily an architectural guide to the islands. Through their buildings, it will provide a glimpse of the long and richly interwoven threads of their history. The illustrations should encourage islander and visitor alike to explore more closely, not only the towns of Kirkwall and Stromness and the better-known buildings and monuments, but also the more obscure sites and especially the outer islands which hold a wealth of interest.

Sequence

This Guide begins in Kirkwall which, as administrative capital for more than eight centuries, holds the key to much that follows. The boundaries of the Mainland parishes are still important community divisions and the Guide adheres to these, beginning in the east with St Andrews, Deerness and Copinsay, and Holm. It then moves to Stromness, the traditional centre for the West Mainland, before following a circuitous route through Sandwick,

A croft near Scapa at the turn of the century

Birsay, Harray, Stenness, Orphir, Firth, Rendall and Evie. From the Mainland it moves to the South Isles which surround Scapa Flow: across the Churchill Barriers to Burray and South Ronaldsay then to Flotta, Hoy and Graemsay. The descriptions of the North Isles begin with those closest to the Mainland: Shapinsay, Rousay, Egilsay and Wyre, then outwards through Stronsay, Sanday, Eday, Westray and Papa Westray to the most northerly, North Ronaldsay. Other, smaller islands have been included where appropriate to the text but not always in line with their parish allegiance.

Text Arrangement
Entries follow the form of name (or street number), address, date and architect. Descriptions of streets and some lesser buildings on them have been incorporated into paragraphs. Where appropriate, illustrations are included of buildings which have been altered or demolished. Text in the small columns relates to historical, less architectural, aspects of the story of Orkney.

Map References
The numbers on the island and town maps refer not to the page numbers but the small numbers adjacent to the description of the building in question.

Access to Buildings
Although a number of the buildings included are open to the public – and those in public ownership are noted as such – many are on private property and this privacy should be respected. Advice on which buildings can be visited and on travel within the islands can be obtained from **Orkney Tourist Board** in Broad Street, Kirkwall, or the Pierhead, S'romness. When crossing farmland visitors should pay due respect to crops and livestock and follow the Country Code.

Sponsors
This Guide would have been impossible had it not been for the kind support of sponsors, pre-eminent amongst them Orkney Islands Council, Occidental Consortium and the Highlands & Islands Development Board, as part of HI Light: the year of the arts. Their generous assistance has helped to lower the cover price of the Guide.

Stromness Town Hall

Thomas Smith Peace (1844-1934)
No name crops up more often than that of T S Peace, not so much because of his skill as an architect but because his career spanned the great era of public building in the late 19th and early 20th centuries and he was given the lion's share of these commissions. After an apprenticeship in his father's wood merchants and construction business he went to Peterhead as a clerk and draughtsman to a builder, then engaged on work at King's College, Aberdeen. Here he came to the notice of Robert Matheson, who as architect to HM Office of Works had superintended the restoration of St Magnus Cathedral. He went to Edinburgh to work on the GPO building, and thence to Matheson's office where he worked alongside draughtsman Charles Doyle, father of the creator of Sherlock Holmes. On returning to Orkney he set up in practice and produced a prodigious amount of work: most notably Kirkwall Town Hall, the Kirkwall Hotel, the Grammar School, and Willowburn Road housing. He was a founder member of the Bowling Club, a Freemason and commodore of Orkney Sailing Club: designing and building his own yacht *Njala*. No other architect before or since has had such a hand in Orkney's built history.

Above *Firth*. Below *Kirkwall 'kloss'*

In 1789 **James Wright** commented that *the streets are long, narrow and dirty in bad weather ... the accommodation for strangers in what they call inns is ... execrable*. Despite this, he was *most agreeably surprised to find collected together in this remote spot of the Kingdom, a most elegant assemblage of Beautiful and Fashionable Females, many of whom would have ornamented the finest assemblies in any of the capitals of Europe*.

The Mainland

When Orcadians refer to the Mainland, they are not talking of mainland Scotland, which is referred to as 'Sooth' or as plain 'Scotland' as if it were a foreign country. Instead, they are describing the largest island of the group whose Norse name was *Hrossey*, horse island, and which is sometimes wrongly referred to as Pomona, due to the misreading of an early map which was merely describing the islands as *fruitful*.

The Mainland is usually described in terms of its eastern and western halves, divided by the narrow neck of land in which Kirkwall is sited. To the east, a low ridge of hills forms the main body of the island with the lower peninsulas of Tankerness and Deerness to the north-east. A second ridge runs westwards from the town, rising to 270m at Mid Hill, the highest point on the Mainland. Another broader ridge runs northwards along the eastern side of the West Mainland. A broad central depression is occupied largely by the lochs of Harray and Stenness while, to the west, the ground rises again to a line of hills and cliffs of up to 100m at the Black Craig and 87m at Marwick Head. On the south-west corner is the long sheltered inlet of Hamnavoe, site of the town of Stromness.

KIRKWALL

Kirkwall is given its first place in history by Rognvald the First, one of the early Norse Earls. The *Orkneyinga Saga* tells us that he *took up residence at Kirkwall and gathered in all the provisions he needed for the winter there*.

Kirkwall from the west, from Barry's
History, 1805

Then was seen the town itself, *out
of which arose like a great mass,
superior in proportion as it seemed to
the whole burgh, the ancient
cathedral of St Magnus, of the
heaviest order of Gothic architecture,
but grand, solemn and stately, the
work of a distant age, and of a
powerful hand.*
Walter Scott, **The Pirate**

He had a great retinue and lived in grand style.
Its Norse name, *Kirkjuvagr* (church on the bay),
implies that the settlement's early origins were
as a religious centre, confirmed by the place-
name Papdale (valley of papae or priests). In
Norse times the church would have been that of
St Olaf, but it is another, much greater church
which has helped give Kirkwall its importance.
It is easy to see the attractions of Kirkwall as a
place of settlement: situated on the mile-wide
isthmus which separates each half of the
Mainland and almost exactly at the centre of
the communications within Orkney. The two
bays of Kirkwall and Scapa provided good
anchorages, and the 'Oyce' or 'Peedie Sea', the
landlocked head of the bay, formed an excellent
natural harbour for shallow-draught Norse
longships.

The Viking village consisted of two straggling
rows of houses at the end of the 'ayre', one
facing the bay and another facing the Oyce. It
was only when another Earl Rognvald came to
power and founded St Magnus Cathedral that
Kirkwall became a centre of any significance.
The influx of ecclesiastical personnel were
accommodated in the area to the south of the
cathedral which, at that time, stood some
distance out of the village on the shore of the
Oyce.

With the removal of the Bishopric from
Birsay, secular power followed, and the town
became a trading centre. In 1486 King James
III granted the charter of a Royal Burgh to
Kirkwall, which secured it special trading
rights. As the town continued to attract new
inhabitants, the space between church and
village was filled up and thus the three
divisions of the medieval town were set: the
original 'Burgh' in the north; the new 'Midtown'
and the ecclesiastical 'Laverock' to the south.
They were linked by a single street, running

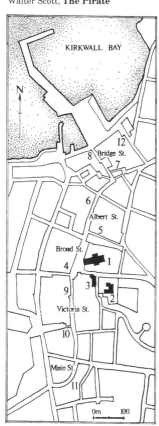

*The centre of Kirkwall by George
Low 1774.*

from north to south, parallel to the shore of the Oyce. In front of St Magnus the street widened to form a market place but for the rest of its length it was a narrow dirt track between two rows of houses built gable-on to the street on long, narrow plots of land.

Kirkwall flourished and, behind the original street, houses and outbuildings were developed, tightly packed with narrow 'klosses' between.

In the 17th and 18th centuries the town became home to a number of wealthy landowners who sought a more elegant style of living than that of the country laird, and through the profits of the kelp boom they could afford it. Like the Baikies, many had large houses in town for the winter months, arranged around off-street courtyards, to provide oases of civilisation in the bustle of the market town.

1 **St Magnus Cathedral**, founded 1137 (see p49) Though St Magnus Cathedral still dominates the skyline of Kirkwall it is not nearly as large a building as its skilful proportion suggests. However, its bold, simple forms and its tall section, more akin to that of continental than British cathedrals, ensure that it is one of the finest and most impressive in Scotland. Despite the extended building period it is notably homogeneous in its design and has a unique colour and warmth; having been constructed with rich red sandstone quarried near Kirkwall and yellow stone from Eday: often used in alternating courses, arches and voussoirs.

In the early 19th century the interior was whitewashed but prior to this the walls and vaults were plastered and painted with designs in red and black: a fragment of which can be seen in the north nave aisle. St Magnus was built by masons who had worked on Durham Cathedral and come north by way of Dunfermline, and the similarities of form and detail are immediately apparent.

The first church, probably in use by the middle of the 12th century, consisted of the present choir. It has the finest Romanesque work north of Durham and set the pattern which was to be followed over the next four centuries, having a three-storey elevation with plain and massive circular piers, broad semicircular arches to lofts at triforium level and clerestory windows above opening across mural passages. The third bay from the crossing is narrower and probably formed an ambulatory passage in front of the shrine of the Martyr which stood in a semicircular apse

Below *St Magnus Cathedral.*
Bottom *South aisle*

St Magnus Cathedral west end and Bishop's Palace

terminating the east end.

The choir aisles have always been vaulted but at first the main roof was an open timber one. In the 13th century the walls were heightened to allow vaulting to be added. At the same time the apse was cleared away and the choir extended eastwards by another three bays to form the present St Rognvald Chapel. These have been constructed in a more elaborate and perhaps French-influenced Transitional style; the moulded columns having subsidiary shafts and capitals carved with foliage, figures and animals. The wooden figures under the east window were designed in 1965 by Stanley Cursiter and executed by Reynold Eunson. They depict Kol, Bishop William and Rognvald, shown holding a model of the Cathedral as it may have been conceived, with eastern apse and twin west towers.

The crossing was rebuilt around 1200: four massive corner pillars with keeled shafts carrying soaring arches decorated with a bold zigzag moulding were inserted into the existing Romanesque work. The lower parts of the transepts which flank it date from the 12th century though the fine South Door is a 13th-century addition and some of the upper parts, particularly the rose window, were heavily reconstructed as late as the 19th century. The Chapels, which open off the transepts, are fine examples of the Transitional style.

Work on the plain Romanesque nave had been progressing slowly from the beginning: the first few columns matching those of the choir with octagonal capitals; the later ones with circular capitals. By the mid-13th century, work on the westward extension of the nave stopped and a temporary gable was erected to allow

The ***Orkneyinga Saga*** tells us that Kali Kolsson, a nephew of the martyred Earl Magnus was given the name Rognvald, half of Orkney and the title of Earl of Sigurd Magnusson, King of Norway (1103-30). However, his first attempt to claim it was defeated by Earl Paul Hakonsson. His father, Kol, suggested that he make a second attempt but this time to vow to build *'a stone minster at Kirkwall more magnificent than any in Orkney'* dedicated to Magnus, endow it with adequate funds and move Magnus's relics and the episcopal seat from Birsay. Whether from saintly intervention or shrewd association with an increasingly popular cult, Rognvald gained his Earldom and kept his promise. The *Orkneyinga Saga* states that *'Kol was principal supervisor of the construction and had the most say in it.'*

The tower is now closed to visitors but **Robert Louis Stevenson** scaled it in 1869: *From every corner of the tower, a corkscrew staircase ascends giving admittance to passages along the blind clerestory of nave, choir and chancel; thence more stairs and narrower passages still – where one has to go sidelong like a crab in a rock cleft – leading along past the little windows of the nave thence more stairs to the dusty and limbered lofts above the groined roof and to the belfry, criss-crossed by great unpainted beams and hung with big bells, on whose narrow sides the modern sacristan rings a stormy chime; and thence by ladder to the outside of the tower.*

Top *St Magnus Cathedral south transept window*. Above *St Rognvald holding model of first cathedral: Stanley Cursiter*

completion of the upper part of the nave. At this stage the nave also was timber roofed and the later addition of the vault caused the pronounced westward lean of the nave piers. The building of the west front had already begun and its three arched portals, though badly weathered, are among the Cathedral's chief glories. Banded with red and yellow stone and shafts with elaborately carved, foliage-decorated capitals, they are topped by pointed arches. Statues may have stood on either side of the larger central doorway while the aisle doors would have been intended to rise into a pair of towers. We can only speculate what the western front might have looked like, but given the quality of the rest of the work, there is little doubt that it would have been spectacular. Instead the Cathedral stood incomplete until at least the late 15th century when the two plainer western bays and the stark west front were completed. Two doors open from the nave aisles: a fine 13th-century Romanesque one to the north and a 16th-century, polygonal-headed exit to Bishop Reid's projected cloister to the south. The vivid stained glass of the west window was designed by Crear McCartney in 1987 to commemorate the 850th anniversary of the founding of the Cathedral.

The tower dates from the early 14th century and, with its tall arched belfry openings, forms an appropriately bold centrepiece to the composition. The bells, were cast in Edinburgh in 1528; the largest being was recast in 1682 after falling to the ground when the tower was struck by lightning. After this it was given a squat pyramidal roof which gave way to the present Gothic, copper-covered spike in 1916 during the restoration under George Mackie Watson. *Open to the public: guidebook available*

2 **Earl's Palace**, Palace Road, 1607
One of the finest Renaissance palaces in Scotland. L-plan in form, the principal chambers are on the first floor above the customary cellars and storerooms. What is unusual is the sheer boldness, scale and quality of its architecture. Larger corner turrets and oriel windows in yellow sandstone corbel out on massive, basket corbels reaching almost to the ground. The broad scale-and-platt stair rises to an exquisite little ante-room perched on an outshot over the service entrance and covered by a carefully moulded vault. Finally, the beautifully proportioned great hall itself has a

tall triple-arched window gable taking up most of the southern gable. One of the corbelled oriels lies in the west wall, while the eastern side has been taken up by two immense bay windows. The bold corbelling suggests a French influence. Earl Patrick's *maister of vark* was Andrew Crawford and his mason, John Ross. *Open to the public: guidebook available.*

Sheriff Court, Palace Road, 1873, David Bryce
The triple window of the first-floor courtroom recalls that in the hall of the adjacent **Earl's Palace**. The suggestion that the palace itself be restored as a replacement for the original 1740 Tolbooth (schemes were produced by Robert Matheson, then working on the Cathedral, and later by Bryce) was never proceeded with. Bryce's original proposals featured a tower over the entrance, abandoned in the executed design which incorporates an advanced chimney gablet over the door, tympanum-headed windows over the courtroom and a tower. The walls incorporate armorial stones salvaged from around the town.

3 **Bishop's Palace**, Palace Road, 12th century (see p 50) The residence of the Bishops of Orkney. A ruined rectangular hall with a round tower at its north-west corner, reconstructed *c.*1550 by Bishop Robert Reid, founder of Edinburgh University.

The lowest courses of rubble stonework match the earliest parts of the adjacent cathedral. Reid's palace had a long hall over a barrel-vaulted basement and the *Moosie Tooer*, which he added, bears his arms and likeness. Inside, a series of roughly square rooms rise to a rectangular cap-house surrounded by a parapet. Earl Patrick Stewart added an extension to the south consisting of an arched loggia with

The Stewart Earls
In 1568 Robert Stewart, illegitimate son of James V, obtained title to the Bishopric Estate and the Earldom of Orkney. He was succeeded in 1593 by his son, Patrick, who developed a reputation which would have done justice to a Medici. Tried and executed in 1615, he was accused of *leaving no sort of extraordinary oppression and treasonable violence unpractised*. He developed a style of living of great extravagance. Whether the vilification of the Earl was justified or whether his attempts to enforce Norse law were seen simply as a threat to the throne is now debated but there is no doubt as to the quality of the architecture which he commissioned both in Orkney and Shetland.

Top left *Earl's Palace, view from the south-east as restored by McGibbon & Ross.* Above *Earl's Palace Chamber*

In 1263 King Haakon Haakonson of Norway died in the palace on his return from defeat at the Battle of Largs and his body was temporarily interred in the Cathedral before being returned to Norway. As he lay on his deathbed he was read the Sagas of the Norse Kings but his passing marked the beginning of the end of their influence in Orkney.

1 Palace Road and 32–36 Broad Street

Other 17th-century houses lined this side of Broad Street into the late 1800s with gables and oriel windows to the street. On the site of the present Town Hall was Bailie William Fea's house: an L-plan two-storey house with tiny attic dormers and a rounded oriel at first-floor level. From it in 1725 Sir James Stewart of Burray and his brother Alexander set out to inflict a beating upon Captain James Moodie of Melsetter in return for a similar indignity suffered at his hands and to it Moodie staggered after being shot in the ensuing scuffle.

Broad Street early 19th century from Hossack's Kirkwall in the Orkneys

massively corbelled turrets to form the *new wark o' the yairds* in combination with his own palace. *Open to the public: guidebook available.* To the south of the Moosie Tooer are **Nos 3-9 Palace Road**, 16th century, a long low two-storey block which was known as the 'Ludging or Long Tenement'. They became a sheltered housing scheme in the 1970s after a Saltire Society award-winning restoration by Orkney County Council and removal of some of the crowstepped projecting outbuildings. The low two-storey **No 26 Broad Street**, 16th century, is said to have served as the Grammar School from 1544 until 1764. Tankerness Lane opposite was known as School Lane, leading down to the sands of the Oyce which served as a playground. In front of the Cathedral is **Broad Street** and the expanse of the **Kirk Green**, Kirkwall's former market place. By contrast with the narrow and dirty 18th-century street, Bishop Pococke judged *the opening before the church ... handsome. The best houses are near it and particularly the town house and jayl.*

Market Cross, 1621

Used for making proclamations and contracts and as a pillory, the original plain stone cross with its engraved date first stood by the foot of the Strynd. It is now in the north transept of the Cathedral, having been replaced this century by a replica. Its most important modern role is as boundary marker and throw-up point for the Ba': a game, open to all-comers, played on New Year's and Christmas Days between the *Doon-the-Gates* (Doonies) and the *Up-the-Gates* (Uppies) who struggle to convey a leather-covered cork ball to their respective ends of the old main street.

Old Tolbooth, 1740, demolished 1890
A gift of £200 from the Earl of Morton, along with permission to take building stone from the ruins of the castle, secured the building of the 18th-century Tolbooth with a prison and guard room on the ground floor, a court room cum council chamber and assembly hall on the first floor and a masonic hall in the attic. On the corner of the Kirk Green at Palace Road, the Broad Street elevation was of some elegance: its five-bayed front having an advanced central gable with an arcade of three semicircular arches at ground level. In requesting permission to convert the Earl's Palace to provide a Sheriff Court and gaol the burgh's eminent petitioners in 1849 suggested that the removal of this 'unsightly, modern building' would open up the view of the Cathedral's western front, although it was another 40 years until its functions were rehoused in more salubrious quarters and it was cleared away.

The Old Tolbooth immediately prior to its demolition in 1890 drawn by T S Peace

4 **Tankerness House**, 16th century (see p 50)
Built as subdeanery and archdeanery for the Cathedral, its two-and-a-half-storey northern wing, gable on to the street with sandstone window surrounds, is associated with Archdeacon Master Gilbert Fulzie, whose initials and arms together with the date 1574 appear on the panel on the corbelled balcony over the arched courtyard gateway. Just inside is a stair tower overlooking the square court formed by the later L-shaped western wing. The

The houses, white with harl, present crowstepped gables to the street; while through an arched gateway, one catches a cool glimpse of a paven entrance court ... the slates are greyish white without the slightest tinge of colour so it is a great relief to the general whiteness of wall and roof to see trees of a decent size spreading in the courts within.
Robert Louis Stevenson, 1869

Tankerness House

house having passed to James Baikie around 1630 and become the town residence of the Baikies of Tankerness, it was considerably rebuilt in the 18th century. In 1968 it was again restored for Kirkwall Burgh Council under Ian G Lindsay & Partners with white render and Caithness slate to form the town's museum, gaining a Civic Trust Commendation. *Open to the public*

The Baikies of Tankerness: James Baikie, 1590-1675, was a successful merchant in Kirkwall who claimed descent from Paul Baikie, pilot to King Haakon in 1264. In around 1630 he gained title to the estate of Tankerness and later to Tankerness House in Kirkwall. He was succeeded by his son, Arthur, who became Provost of Kirkwall, beginning the long involvement of Baikies in the public life of the burgh. James Baikie's descendants owned the Hall of Tankerness until 1951.

Town Hall, 1884, T S Peace
To house the town council chambers, a public hall, post office, free library and offices for the municipal officials, Kirkwall's most prolific architect produced a three-storey Baronial edifice to face the Cathedral: a rather timid one by comparison with the robust examples of the original style nearby. A tall advanced gable over the entrance is flanked by the slender cone-roofed bartizans with a small castellated tower to the right. The main door is flanked by fluted freestone columns, topped by statues. The whole elevation is enlivened with heavy mouldings and assorted armorial stones. The building was renovated in its centenary year by Orkney Islands Council to form a Community Centre with a timber-lined interior which manages to combine a degree of Victorian civic exuberance with modern comfort. The original hall has a curving roof with Ionic pilasters and colourful stencilled decoration.

No 5 Broad Street, 18th century
A two-storey L-plan house round a courtyard which has a low wall and tall gateposts to the street topped with an iron arch and railings. Its wood-panelled rooms housed John Riddoch who, in the 18th century, was the Sheriff-Substitute and built the house on the site of the Castle's south block-house.

Kirkwall Castle, *c.*1380
Earl Henry St Clair, a Scotsman of Norman descent, was granted the earldom by King Haco VI of Norway in 1379. Although he had agreed to build no fort without royal assent, he immediately did. The Castle stood until 1615 when, along with the Girnel, the Palace and the Cathedral tower, it was taken over by supporters of Earl Patrick during his imprisonment. As a result, the Castle was destroyed and the last remnants cleared away in 1865 to make way for Castle Street, leaving only a well under the middle of the road and a small heraldic stone and commemorative plaque on the wall of the former Castle Hotel (now the Trustee Savings Bank).

Masonic Hall, Castle Street, 1885, T S Peace
A rusticated sandstone ground floor with large windows is topped by an upper storey in dressed flagstone. A heavy cornice is arched over the door to form a pediment with masonic symbols while the window above has a triangular pediment.

Below 5 Broad Street. Bottom Ruins of the castle before removal drawn by T S Peace

Burgher

Orkney Library

The Earl of Caithness landed with *ane great cannon callit thrawn mouthe* and *commanded the cannoneers to shute at the castle, who did their part so well that by the second shot one of the turrets upon the head of the house was pierced and almost beaten down*, although he was *to protest to God the house has never been biggit without the consent of the divil for it is one of the strongest houses in Britain – without fellow.*

Castleyards, 1982, Orkney Islands Council
Architects: M M Gilbertson, R G Dewar
A rather conscious attempt to recreate the
character of the old town centre this group of
council flats and houses, with its profusion of
gables and harling, manages to retain the
streetline and forms a sunny courtyard.
The position of the original Castleyards is
marked by **Nos 4-8 Broad Street**, early 19th
century, three-bayed Georgian houses. **No 4**,
with its elegant pilastered and corniced door,
now houses the Tourist Office. Two-storeyed
with a dormered attic it has a wing and stair
tower to the rear.

5 **The Strynd**, originally called the King's
Passage, is a narrow flagstone-paved lane
between two high, possibly medieval, dry-stone
walls. In the Second World War it was roofed
over as the town's air raid shelter. The row of
four low, two-storey houses, 1703, on the north
side of the street were renovated in 1979 by
Orkney Islands Council with white render and
Caithness slate roofs. A freestone-arched pend
leads into their back gardens to the west. The
second house down, built by Andrew Morrison,
a church treasurer, was visited by William IV
(before his accession) in 1785. It later became
the manse of the secession church whilst the
top one was simultaneously a cathedral manse.
No record exists of relations between these
neighbours.

Top *4-8 Broad Street*. Above *Strynd*.

Albert Street (see p 50) runs north from Broad
Street, still retaining many of the houses gable
on to the street which give it much of its
character – their long narrow gardens formerly
running down to the Oyce to the west and up
the hill to the east. Its most distinctive feature
is the famous **Big Tree**, now sadly reduced to a
tall stump, which once stood within a garden
wall, removed in the 19th century for street
widening. Despite the oft-repeated joke that
this is the only tree in Orkney, Kirkwall
gardens are well endowed with trees: mainly
sycamores. **No 59**, the 18th-century two-and-a-
half-storey 'double tenement', whose garden
this was, has a long rendered and painted
frontage to the street and three gabled dormers.
It was, in 1762, the birthplace of the historian
Malcolm Laing.

59 Albert Street

43 Albert Street, 17th century
A pair of two-storey houses with painted
window surrounds form an L-shape round an

After joining the summer tours in 1866 and 1867, arranged by the Commissioners for Northern Lights, **William Chambers** wrote of Kirkwall:

I was more pleased with it than with any other town of its size I had seen for a long time. It is clean, neat, old fashioned. The narrow streets ... are lined with buildings of the style of the 17th century when Scottish domestic architecture was distinguished for its picturesque tastefulness. Instead therefore of the bald frontages of the 18th century we find in Kirkwall the tapering crow-stepped gables, the ornamental gateways with heraldic insignia and the small quadrilateral courtyards which characterise the era of the later Stewarts. In these well-preserved specimens of an interesting style of architecture we see the dwellings of the Orcadian gentry in past times, and yet not altogether past – for till this day, the houses I speak of are mostly occupied by a respectable order of families – not degraded by an invasion of paupers from all quarters of the kingdom, as is unhappily the case with the old mansions in Edinburgh. But besides these antique buildings, Kirkwall exhibits traces of modern prosperity and taste, including the erection of a new hotel, the opening of new thoroughfares and the erection of handsome villas in the neighbourhood.

attractive courtyard opening on to the street. The gable of the front house leaves just enough space for modern traffic to pass and demonstrates the former constriction of the street. The rear house has a moulded doorcase and a pend leading through to **No 45** which has a pilastered sandstone porch. **No 34 Albert Street** (Hourston's) has a 19th-century elegant sandstone frontage to a high timber-lined interior with wide arched windows and a gabled door canopy bearing the Burgh's motto: *Si Deus Nobiscum.*

6 **Custom House**, 33 Albert Street, *c.*1830
The white painted Custom House presents a narrow frontage with two full storeys and another under its piended roof with a central dormer. The colourful Royal Arms of Scotland and large lettering provide functional decoration. Originally built as an extension to the house of Captain William Balfour RN of Elwick.

Top right *Broad Street to the pier – note the trees!* Below *45 Albert Street.* Right *Custom House, 33 Albert Street*

Kirkwall Library, Laing Street, 1908, J Malcolm Baikie

This symmetrical two-storey building in dressed flagstone represents the third scheme which Baikie produced. The first had a tall central castellated tower. The second, much reduced, had an optional castellated or classical dress. In the end the present simple three-bayed arrangement with sandstone classical portico and pedimented upper windows was constructed, and remodelled in 1963 with local stone extensions by the County Architect, A T Jamieson.

Albert Hotel, Mounthoolie Lane, late 19th century; renovated 1987-9, L E Sparrow

Disparate elements of dressed stone hotel building and its later bar and hall have been pulled together in a lively renovation which gives the resulting entertainment complex an architectural presence which these plain buildings never achieved before. The mansarded nightclub entrance takes an irreverent cue from the nearby Kirkwall Hotel.

No 8 Albert Street (Hydro Electric), c.1863, David Rhind

Originally the Commercial Bank, this three-storey Italianate mini-palazzo in Orkney stone, with round-headed windows and overhanging eaves, was designed by the architect of the Bank's Head Office in George Street, Edinburgh.

Albert Street ends where the old main street crossed the bridge over the Papdale Burn. Originally the crossing to the south-east corner of St Ola's kirkyard, it was demolished in the 19th century when the burn was culverted. Its parapet stone bears the burgh arms and the date 1682, and is preserved in the façade of the Town Hall.

Bridge Street leads north from here to the harbour. This is the oldest part of the town and marks the original shore of the Oyce.

7 St Olaf's Kirk, 11th century

A heavily moulded sandstone Romanesque archway rebuilt in St Olaf's Wynd is one of the few remnants of the original 'Kirk on the Bay'. Two ogee-headed aumbries have been removed to the Victorian Episcopal Church which also takes the name of the Norwegian king from 1015 to 1030, Olaf Haraldson.

Kirkwall has the oldest public library in Scotland, established in 1683, following the donation of a collection of mostly theological books by William Baikie of Holland. Having been housed in the Cathedral, Tolbooth and then the Town Hall, the Kirkwall Free Library was growing rapidly at the turn of the century and money for a new building came from Andrew Carnegie who visited Kirkwall to open it.

Albert Street was crossed by the course of an open ditch known as the *long gutter* now marked by Laing Street and the narrow Mounthoolie Lane. In 1703 the *haill inhabitants* were ordered to *cleanze and dight the long gutter* which was *bagd up with gutter and other filthines.*

The small court which preceded the Commercial Bank was known as Parliament Close and it was here that Orkney's own parliament administered, under the Earl, the Scandinavian laws which remained in force after the mortgaging of the islands. In 1611 during the trial of Patrick Stewart the Privy Council decreeed that *the subjects of this kingdom should live and be governit under the lawis and statutes of this realm allenarly ... and discharges the said foreign lawis to be no further usit within the said counties of Orknay and Zetland* but Parliament Close remained the centre of public business well into the 17th century.

Commercial Bank at the turn of the century

T Kent - Orkney Library

Drawing of Aumbry from St Olaf's Church by T S Peace

Walter Scott dined at William Scollay's original Ship Inn here on 12 August 1814 and Hossack suggests that it was the lack of a formal welcome by the inhabitants such as he received in Shetland that caused him to pen his famous description of 'fair Kirkwall' as:

A base little burgh, both dirty and mean,
There's nothing to do and naught to be seen
Save a church where of old times a prelate harangued
And a palace that's built by an Earl that was hanged.

Bridge Street – Ship Inn on the right

21 Bridge Street (Jolly's), 18th century
With a two-and-a-half-storey gable to the street, this building has been recently restored and a narrow court cleared to the south with a stone-built porch.

Folly, 1830
Built in the garden of James Traill of Woodwick's town house in the year he became provost, this summer house is a small square building with a tall conical spire constructed with the volcanic ballast from Pirate Gow's ship after it went aground on the Calf of Eday.

Nos 6-12 Bridge Street, 20th century
Built as the shops and stores of James Flett & Sons, General Merchants, and occupied as such until the 1970s; the northernmost shop has a timber-galleried interior and open-trussed roof with skylights. **No 5** Bridge Street (Ship Inn) is a 17th-century, three-storey, crowstepped building gable to the street, its upper windows, rearranged in a central position, with segmental-arched heads.

Kirkwall Hotel, Harbour Street, 1890, T S Peace
The four-storey backdrop to the Basin is the solid bulk of William Dunnet's hotel in dressed local stone with sandstone mouldings topped by mansard roofs and dormered windows. Crude Corinthian columns flank the door topped by a low, wide pediment. Workmanlike rather than elegant, it still forms a successful culmination to the narrow main street heightening the contrast with the open harbour front.

Kirkwall Harbour
Passengers and goods arriving in Kirkwall prior to 1811 had to be decanted into small boats to go ashore on the 'ayre'. At that date the east pier at the end of Bridge Street was finished and work on the west pier began two years later. The east pier was extended around 1830 and during 1865-7 a new iron pier was erected to designs by R Denison. This in turn was supplanted by a more substantial stone pier in 1886 designed by John D Millar. At the time of writing it is undergoing extension to see it into the next century.

Girnel, Harbour Street, 17th century
The long, low storehouse for grain paid as rental to the Earldom estate stands above the Corn Slip

with two rubble-walled storeys and an attic. A double forestair provides access to the first floor. The two-storey **Girnel Keeper's House**, 1643, stands next to it, gable on to the harbour and separated by a narrow lane which has been built over with a door headed by an elegant fanlight.

Robert Louis Stevenson viewed the new iron pier in 1869: *A London engineer has erected an iron jetty like the ornamental bridge over the water in a cockney tea garden. A gimcrack lane of corner lamp posts, infinitely neat and infinitely shaky – a nursemaid's walk that might have done at Greenwich, projecting into the easterly surge from the Mainland of Orkney. Alas! Alas!*

Top *Kirkwall Pier, c.1870 drawn by T S Peace.* Left *The Girnel, Kirkwall.*

Ayre Hotel, 1791
Formerly two houses, built on reclaimed land at the inner end of the 'ayre', the natural spit which separates the 'Peedie Sea' from the Bay. Two-storey with later gabled dormers to an attic floor and flat-roofed porches, the white rendered group is a distinctive landmark on the seafront. The eastern house was the home of James Erskine, merchant, who built them both, while the western one was the last town house of the Stewarts of Brough, Westray and later of the Traills of Holland in Papa Westray. Between the Ayre Hotel and the row of four 19th-century two-storey **houses** running back towards the 'Peedie Sea' is a low single-storey range with a splayed semicircular sandstone archway in its seaward gable. This was formerly the entrance to Kirkwall's first **East Church of Scotland** which was constructed in 1841 in the vicinity of the present St Magnus Hall. However, in 1843 following the Disruption, its congregation joined the Free

Ayre Hotel and Shed Gables

Kirkwall Post Office

Church and were evicted by the Church of Scotland. Its materials were sold to James Walls who used them to build this row.

Junction Road and **Great Western Road** have both been constructed on land reclaimed from the Oyce. The former was built in 1865, along with Castle Street, in order to open up the approach to the harbour.

Kirkwall Post Office, Junction Road, 1960, Ministry of Public Buildings & Works
A long harled block, with square upper windows, its simple geometry, plain sandstone window surrounds and modern relief carving of a Viking ship over the door do more to echo vernacular building traditions than any number of crowsteps.

Ayre Mills, 19th century
Originally the Oyce mouth was open and the flow of the tide was harnessed in 1839 by Thomas Platt with a wheel, adjustable to rise and fall with the tide, which powered a saw mill. It later became a meal mill and was at different times powered by steam, gas and diesel, formerly having a square brick chimney behind it. The building is a long three-storey range with a double block of stores flanked by crowstepped kilns, the eastern one dated 1868, and with 19th century houses at either end. The tidal wheel was housed in wooden shed to west.

Hatston Airfield, 1939
As HMS *Sparrowhawk* in the Second World War, this Fleet Air Arm base was the first in Britain to have hard runways. After the war, it served as the civil airport for a time while its wooden huts were used as council housing up to the 1970s. The pitched-roofed hangars have become the basis of the town's industrial estate and one blocky 1930s-style building with large metal corner windows and a flat roof remains.

Grain Earth House, Hatston, *c.*500BC
It is thought that this structure served as an underground food store for a settlement above. A curving stone-lined passage slopes downward into an oval chamber whose roof is carried on four long, thin stones set on end, with similar stones acting as lintels. The walls are of dry-stone construction. *Open to the public*

Glaitness Primary School, Pickaquoy Road, 1979 Orkney Islands Council Architects:

In 1942 the Ayre Mills *(above)* became home to **Orkney Egg Producers Ltd** and in the years 1950-1 almost 100 million eggs were graded, packed and exported from here. Up until 1952 the countryside was littered with small black wooden hen houses engaged in what had become Orkney's biggest industry, sustaining many smaller crofts. In that year, the islands were hit by a 125 mph hurricane which carried many of the hens and houses out to sea. The industry picked itself up but never reached the same peak and was gradually killed off by its distance from markets and battery farming in the south.

M M Gilbertson and R Barnes
Domestic in style and scale with a pitched, plain-tiled roof; its peripheral classrooms open into communal areas. The theme has been continued in the extension **Aurrida House**, 1989-90, Orkney Islands Council Architects: L E Sparrow

Victoria Street is the continuation of the old main street south from the Kirk Green and has come under less development pressure than the more commercial Albert Street. Gables project on to the narrow and irregular street, many with chamfered corners, more with crowsteps and all two or three storeys high.

With a plain gable to the street, **Nos 12-14 Victoria Street** (Jolly's), 17th century, was the town house of Arthur Baikie of Sound, Shapinsay, through whose daughter it passed to the Buchanans. In 1819 Peter Calder bought it and turned it into the principal hostelry in the town. The painted façade of **No 15**, 19th century, is topped by a pair of dormers and brings a bright counterpoint to the grey street. **Nos 19-25**, *c.*1810, a long, low five-bay block fronting the street, has elaborate scrolled putt stones and a marriage lintel bearing the date 1743 has been incorporated from the house of Robert Mackay and Margaret Mowat which stood on the site before it. **Nos 33-41**, 17th century, present a group of four gables with closes between them in the original style while one of Kirkwall's most elaborate marriage lintels is preserved opposite at **No 34**. Carved in red sandstone, it commemorates the wedding of John Traill and Helen Stewart in 1769 and is decorated with foliage and birds.

Walls' Close leads to a group of rendered council houses, 1981, Orkney Islands Council Architects: M M Gilbertson and G MacDonald Slotted into the long gardens behind Victoria Street. A combination of new and restored buildings which ties in with the surrounding buildings by use of small-scale public spaces and routes leading between them. The south side of **Gunn's Close** is made up of a row of 17th-century two-storey houses, traditional with local slate roofs and brightly painted.

No 60 Victoria Street, 17th century, has a low rubble-built gable projecting into the street with a tall central chimney and a doorway set in the chamfered and corbelled ground-floor corner. Behind the tall three-storey block of

9

10

Victoria Street: Nos. 19-25 on the right

Near the present-day Royal Hotel was born **Sir Robert Strange** (1721-92) who achieved fame in London as an engraver of Renaissance paintings. He served with Charles Edward Stewart in the '45 and at one stage is said to have evaded capture in Edinburgh's Fleshmarket Close by hiding under his lover's hooped skirts.

Walls' Close

Gunn's Close view from west

No 64 is a pleasant courtyard surrounded by low rubble-walled buildings, one with a forestair.

Spence's Square, 72-74 Victoria Street, 17th century, is a small court with a screen wall and formerly an arched gateway to the street. The northern house, gable to the road has decorated skewputts: one bearing a clerical-looking head in flat Geneva cap and ruff, identified with a Revd William Scott, minister of the Cathedral and resident here in *c.*1725. The rear houses have first-floor entrances with a linking

Right Courtyard behind 64 Victoria Street. Below Decorated putt stone, Spence's Square. Bottom Spence's Square

walkway over a close which leads to the back gardens. The whole square has undergone award-winning restoration by Orkney Islands Council with white render and Caithness slates. Victoria Street's two public buildings are the discreet **Gospel Hall**, 1880, and the bulky **Baptist Church**, 1888 (formerly the UP Hall), both by T S Peace. The latter has a broad frontage with semicircular windows and a gabled porch with an inscription over.

Clay Loan breaks the old main street, climbing steeply to Gallow Ha': the former place of public execution. Originally the Common or South Loan, it takes its name from its use as a source of mortar for Kirkwall houses. The entrance to Victoria Street is flanked by the chamfered and corbelled corners of **Nos 6** and **8 Clay Loan**, the latter, 17th century, a low two-storeys with flat-topped dormers prised up from the local slate roof.

Main Street is the continuation of the old street which curved around the southern 'foot' of the Oyce, leading to the old roads to Scapa and the West Mainland. Tall 18th-century houses flank the entrance.

11 **West End Hotel,** 14 Main Street, 1824
Fronting the street on the south-east with a
more recent cast-iron balcony, this tall three-
storey, four-bay house, was built for Captain
William Richan of Rapness. In 1845 it became
the first Balfour Hospital thanks to a bequest
made by John Balfour of Trenaby. Richan's wife
was famed for her extravagance and was once
reputed to have used a £50 note as a sandwich
filling in order to win a wager by eating the
most expensive breakfast. **No 20 High Street**,
c.1880, T S Peace, is a low stone pavilion with
piended slate roofs (in the garden behind),
constructed as the fever hospital.

West End Hotel and Main Street

Our Lady's Catholic Church, 1877
A plain dressed-stone chapel with priest's house
attached, it has recently been re-oriented with
the altar moved into the northern octagonal end.
It features a powerful set of carved wooden
Stations of the Cross by Marvin Elliott. The gable
of the house opposite is the Uppies' Ba' goal.

Wellington Street and **High Street** continued
the town westward in the 18th century with
mostly two-storey houses fronting the southern
side of the street. Hossack records that Burgar's
Bay, *an unsavoury recess* about half-way up
Wellington Street, was the Uppies' Ba' goal,
while a lane running from it to Clay Loan was
known as *Neukatineuks*.

Andersquoy, Old Scapa Road, 1880s, T S Peace
The 'County Home' has a large central stone block
with part piended roof, projecting rafter ends and
gabled dormers, flanked by single-storey wings,
giving the external appearance of a large villa. Its
extension, **St Rognvald's House**, 1975, Moira &
Moira, features shallow monopitch roofs and felt-
covered walls suggesting a modern Scandinavian
influence. The **Malcolm Gilbertson Memorial
Day Centre**, 1987, Orkney Islands Council
Architects: L E Sparrow, is a low pavilion with a
shallow gambrel roof in red tiles and full-height
glazed walls to the south. A pair of houses link it
in form to the 'pavilions' of the old building.

Andersquoy

Garden Memorial Building, Balfour
Hospital, New Scapa Road, 1924, T S Peace
A low-rendered building with piended slate
roofs; its moulded door surround is topped by a
small gable and flanked by outlying pavilions.
The hospital has since undergone considerable
extension.

Cromwell Road *(see p 50)* takes its name from the site of one of two forts built in Cromwell's time, thanks to the efforts of Morton and Montrose in the Royalist cause. The English soldiers were no respecters of Kirkwall's architectural heritage, using pews from the Cathedral and the churchyard dyke as sources of materials. In return they are credited with the introduction of cabbage and venereal disease to the islands.

¹² **Shore Street** used to be backed by a line of gables facing the sea: the ends of the rows of 17th- and 18th-century houses which made up Erskine's Court, with the Long Close leading up from the shore and Thwart Close crossing into St Catherine's Place. These were lined with low two-storey, rubble-built houses with local slate roofs having dormers peeled up from the edges. The whole area, though surveyed for redevelopment in 1924, was later cleared away for an oil depot.

The eastern side of **St Catherine's Place**, *c.*1805, consists of similar ranges of two storey houses, gable to the street with flagstone closes between, which were constructed as workers' houses by a farmer, Andrew Drever.

Berstane Road is made up mainly of detached villas and bungalows. **Daisybank**, East Road, 18th century, is a square-plan, plain Georgian house with a shallow piended Caithness slate roof, large central chimneys in line with the ridge and a classical doorcase: a house type commonly used for manses in Orkney. To the rear is a single-storey crowstepped wing with a dormered loft.

Below *St Catherine's Place*
Below right *Shore Street in the early 20th century.* Bottom *St Catherine's Place.* Bottom right *Erskine Court (off St Catherine's Place)*

The Long Close in 1924

Papdale House,Berstane Road,
late 18th century
Visited by Scott in 1814 when he called on his
'old acquaintance' Malcolm Laing. Two-
storeyed, three-bayed and harled with
sandstone window surrounds it has a
pedimented projecting centre gable with an
oculus which overlooks its estate in the Papdale
Valley. To the south-east is an 18th-century,
large, walled garden with a square corner
tower.

Park Cottage, Berstane Road, 19th century
A striking design, its single storey has a
pyramidal Caithness slate roof rising to a tall
central chimney stack and pierced by long, low,
heavily corniced dormers. **Alton House,**
Berstane Road, 18th century, is an upright,
rendered two-storey house with an advanced
centre bay, sandstone window surrounds and
piended roof.

Orkney Islands Council Offices, School
Place, *c.*1890, T S Peace
The former Kirkwall Grammar School, this is
Peace's most distinguished building, developed
from an original, low, stone, H-shaped block,
symmetrical about its modern front door and
dominated by its bulky steep-roofed bell tower.
It is enlivened by gables with stepped ends to
the skews, topped by low pinnacles and fronted
by oculi. It has been heightened and extended
by a two-storey wing to the rear. The building
replaced the 1820 school, designed by a Mr
Gillespie, which was a low pavilion with a

Malcolm Laing (1762-1818) was an
advocate and later the author of
A History of Scotland while his
brother Samuel Laing (1780-1868)
translated the *Heimskringla* and was
in the forefront of agricultural
improvement, notably at Stove in
Sanday. Both were prominent in
local affairs: it was Malcolm who
saved the remaining Standing Stones
of Stenness from demolition while
Samuel was Provost of Kirkwall and
his son, also Samuel, became MP for
the Northern Burghs.

Papdale House

The Grammar School probably began as the Cathedral's 'Sang School' teaching *music, manners and virtue* to choristers as well as Latin. The first recorded schoolmaster was Thomas Houston who was appointed by Bishop Reid to hold office from 1544 to 1595. The Grammar School has an enviable record of famous alumni and it is often remarked that one of Orkney's greatest exports is professors.

The old Grammar School and 6-10 School Place

piended roof and arched doorway. In 1818, work on a new school had actually begun in the Cathedral Churchyard, when Sheriff Peterkin had an inderdict slapped on it to prevent what Hossack described as *the well-meaning local goths from rearing an incongruous pile against the venerable walls of the ancient church*. In 1980, the building underwent a slightly claustrophobic conversion into a modern council headquarters. Three floors were fitted into the former two storeys of high-ceilinged classrooms with discreet lead-covered additions in intervening spaces.

East Church, 1847

The Paterson Church, named after its minister from 1820 to 1870, is a massive, galleried preaching-barn capable of accommodating over a thousand. It is fronted by a tripartite ashlar gable with a large traceried, arched window and topped by pyramidal pinnacles resting on a series of columns. On 12 September 1883 W E Gladstone and Alfred Tennyson were given the freedom of the burgh in this former UP church. It now serves as a second Church of Scotland, in addition to the Cathedral.

The area to the east of the church in the Papdale Valley was developed largely as council housing in this century. The first of these was **Willowburn Road** in 1921 by T S Peace, a curve of rendered semi-detached Arts & Crafts-inspired houses with roofs sloping out over the projecting bays which contain their front doors.

East Church

In 1921 Building Industries congratulated Peace on *the excellent and useful manner in which he has designed the dwellings in question – each house will contain a living room, three bedrooms, a scullery, a bathroom, a larder and a coal place.*

Papdale Mill, 1856, altered by T S Peace

A long stone building, heightened to three storeys in 1880, it was again altered around 1890 and given a massive 8m square kiln with a pyramidal roof to one side.

Papdale Primary School, 1961,
A T Jamieson, County Architect
Festival of Britain in style, flat-roofed, rational
planning dressed up with local Walliwall stone. A
jagged row of classrooms looks south-west across
the playing fields from a large expanse of glazing
while the hall stands separated on the town side.

Papdale Primary School

Dundas Crescent is a sweeping curve of late-
19th-century local stone villas. **Rognvalsay** and
Raey House are good examples: the former,
symmetrical with bay windows flanking its
entrance; the latter L-plan with bay windows,
porch and barge-boarded gables and dormers.

Below *St. Olaf's Church and Rectory.* Bottom *Laing Brae*

St Olaf's Church, 1874-5, Alexander Ross
Kirkwall's Episcopal Church by Inverness' great
Episcopal architect stands in spacious grounds
beside its two-storey rectory, presenting a low-
sided, steeply pitched dressed flagstone gable
with a tripartite window to the street. The
entrance porch was later extended upwards to
form a blunt square tower with a pyramid roof
in honour of Archdeacon J B Craven: incumbent
from the founding of the building until 1914
and author of *A History of the Church in
Orkney*. The church contains two aumbreys
from the original St Olaf's Church, woodwork
from Bishop Graham's Episcopal gallery and
throne in the Cathedral and a rough stone font
from St Mary's Chapel at Swandro, Rousay.

Laing Brae, Bignold Park Road, 1862, is a
particularly attractive spreading single-storey
cottage with bay windows, a low piended slate
roof and a gablet over the door.

Bignold Park Pavilion, 1910, J Malcolm
Baikie, is an elegant white-rendered two-storey
sports pavilion presenting a balcony with
elaborate iron supports and railings, and three
large dormers to the playing fields.

Above *Bignold Park Pavilion*. Right *Highland Park Distillery*

Buckham Hugh Hossack (1836-1902) was born in Stronsay but spent his working life as a teacher in Edinburgh before retiring to Orkney at a relatively young age. He was widely involved in local politics and voluntary organisations but is best remembered for his *Kirkwall in the Orkneys* which, house by house, recorded the history of the burgh and through it, the islands. Although 90 years old it is still a standard reference work without which no Orkney book could be written.

Below *Craigiefield*. Bottom *Berstane House*

13 **Highland Park Distillery**, Holm Road, 19th century

A long series of low, bonded warehouses in local stone with slate roofs and a pair of pagoda-shaped ventilation towers are the most distinctive features of this complex which was established in 1798. The offices and other older buildings around the iron archway, which marks the entrance to the distillery proper, were restored in 1987 to form a visitors' centre. *Open to the public*

ST OLA

The parish which surrounds Kirkwall takes its name from the 'Church on the Bay' which founded the burgh.

Craigiefield, *c.*1880, T S Peace

A broad stone house with a part-piended slate roof and matching porch, it employs Peace's favourite motif of the time – the projecting rafter end – and was built for B H Hossack who shared Peace's interests in sailing and freemasonry.

Berstane House, 1850, David Bryce

Built for William Balfour, younger brother of David who commissioned **Balfour Castle**, Shapinsay; its organisation is almost identical to Balfour and **Trumland** with principal rooms on the first floor looking out over Inganess Bay and a corner drawing room leading to a conservatory. The plain, picturesque villa realisation could not be more different, however, with semi-octagonal bays covered by projecting gabled roofs and the ground floor sunk down to reduce the scale still further.

Harbour Building, Scapa, 1980, Orkney Islands Council Architects: M M Gilbertson
This pyramidal 'mushroom', with large windows peering out of its plain tiled roof, is the control centre for the waters around Scapa Flow.

Foveran, 1976
A low harled and tiled guest house with projecting restaurant windows and a relaxed and comfortable timber-lined interior.

Caldale Airship Station, (above)
Old Finstown Road, 1917
Although nothing now remains of the site that is recognisable as the large arched hangars of this base, there are remains of the camp huts. The balloons were sheltered by movable wind-screens and, as well as airships, the base was home to reconnaissance balloons carried by warships which were inflated here and towed by lorry to Scapa Pier or, round Wideford Hill, to Kirkwall.

Top *Harbour Office.* Middle *Scapa Pier with salt 'cuithes'.* Above *Wideford Hill Cairn*

14 **Wideford Hill Cairn**, *c.*2500BC
High on a hillside, this communal tomb has a narrow entrance and a 2m high rectangular corbelled chamber with three side cells opening off it. The outside of the cairn has been exposed by quarrying and shows series of circular walls.
Open to the public: guidebook available

EAST MAINLAND: ST ANDREWS
Sloping down from the central spine of moorland across a broad low-lying peninsula, St Andrews makes up the northern half of the

East Mainland and is divided into the districts of Tankerness in the north and Toab in the south-east. Rising barely above 40m it contains the only sizeable body of fresh water in the East Mainland: the Loch of Tankerness.

15 **Battery**, Rerwick Road, Tankerness
The remains of a camp and battery of 6-in. coastal defence guns whose mountings survive, inside two large concrete emplacements. A two-storey observation tower stands behind with concrete bunkers for searchlights, a generator shed and concrete bases marking the positions of huts. Cantilevered concrete roofs on a separate steel structure and stepped details at openings unconsciously prefigure the work of more modern architects.

16 **Hall of Tankerness**, *c.*1550; altered
The original part of the present house is the long two-storey southern wing, which was built for the Groats of Tankerness before passing to James Baikie around 1630. In the 19th century a broad single-storey corrugated iron pavilion with an encircling veranda was added to the north-east linked by a conservatory. It forms the present main body of the house having been rebuilt in more substantial form and given an additional floor in 1910. To the west of this a kitchen court is bounded by sheds and offices making up a curving castellated screen wall with Gothic arched windows, peeling away from the old house and terminating in a low round tower.

Burial Vault, Hall of Tankerness
A stone-built, barrel-vaulted remnant of the old St Andrews Chapel, covered by a slightly

Top Searchlight mounting and generator shed, Rerwick. Above Rerwick Battery, detail

Hall of Tankerness

*Left Hall of Tankerness.
Below Burial vault*

curving pitched flagstone roof; the burial place
of the Baikie family.

Fishing Station, Tankerness, 19th century
A broad stone pier with central wooden bollards
and an upended cannon at its extremity. At its
head stands three two-storey buildings which
housed those engaged in the herring industry;
the central one distinguished by arched gable
doorways. The New Statistical Account records
that in Tankerness *the curing of the herring
commenced with us only in 1833.*

Tankerness Meal Mill, mid 19th century
Tall elegant round-headed arches, now built up,
mark the original position of the water wheel.
The undershot wheel which replaced it was
built into the end wall and contained by a
screen wall to avoid frightening horses on the
adjacent bridge.

Old Manse, 1756
A minister's elegant residence with tripartite
window heightened to two and a half storeys in
1793, and again altered in 1830; now semi-
derelict.

North Church, 1801; altered 1827 and *c.*1915
Buttressed walls, traceried window in the east
and an oculus and belfry with weather vane in
the west: more elaborate than most of Orkney's
Presbyterian churches.

Tankerness Meal Mill

DEERNESS
Deerness is a roughly quadrilateral peninsula
joined to the eastern corner of St Andrews by a
narrow sandy strip at Dingieshowe. Although
gently sloping and fertile it rises to 48m cliffs at
Mull Head in the north. To the east the cliffs
are pierced by a cave whose inner end has
collapsed, leaving a 20m-deep chasm with an
archway open to the sea known as the 'Gloup'.
Low remnants of chapel walls and other

The Covenanters' Memorial, 19th century, is a stone-built pillar on the clifftop, commemorating 250 drowned covenanters whose pledge to aid the abolition of English episcopacy had led to their capture at Bothwell Bridge in 1679. Sent for transportation, their ship was carried from its moorings on to Mull Head. There were 50 survivors, no thanks to the crew who battened down the hatches and pushed many of those who did make it ashore back into the water. The monument was erected at the instigation of a South American visitor to Orkney.

Above *Braebuster*. Right *Point of Mirkady, fishing station.* Below *Deerness Church: sketch by Rev George Low, 1774*

foundations remain of the 12th-century Brough of Deerness.

Braebuster, 1888
A tall, picturesque villa in local stone with sandstone dressings, built for Samuel Reid, Provost of Kirkwall.

Horse Mill, Mirkady, 19th century
A circular stone horse-gang with conical slate roof which powered a threshing mill; inside, a radiating timber roof structure and massive timber cross beam for carrying the machinery. 17 The contemporary **Fishing Station** is a two-storey stone block with a lean-to shed and external end stair overlooking the point of Mirkady. Herring fishing in Deerness supported 50-60 boats in the mid 19th century.

18 **St Ninian's Church**, Skaill, 1798
Plain with round-arched windows and a pyramid-roofed belfry it was built on the site of a *pretty ancient* building with twin cap-roofed circular towers, depicted by Low in 1774. It takes its present name from SS *St Ninian* which went ashore in the bay in 1903.

Copinsay Lighthouse, 1915,
David A Stevenson
Three km south-east of Deerness, the wedge-shaped island of Copinsay rises to cliffs of over 70m, which are home to thousands of birds. The stubby 16m tower of the lighthouse, with a two-level external balcony and shallow black-domed roof, squats behind the massive cliff-edge bulwark which supports its foghorn.

HOLM
Lying along the north-eastern edge of Scapa Flow and reaching 100m at Gaitnip, Holm slopes down northwards towards the moorland

centre of the East Mainland and southwards to green and lower-lying ground around Holm Sound.

19 St Mary's

A former fishing village comprising a row of mostly 19th-century two-storey cottages straggling along the landward side of the shore road above a long pier. Its importance as a harbour disappeared with the construction of the Barriers in the Second World War.

Storehouse, 1608

A 'girnel' for the Meil Estate, standing by the shore: two storeys, a loft and steeply pitched crowstep gables.

20 Graemeshall, 1874 and 1896

The two-storey southern wing with its dormered attic replaced the 16th-century house of Meil, a single-storey building with two external stairs. To the north lay a courtyard which corresponded to the position of the present southern wing. A new two-storey house with attic was erected in 1626 to form the north side of the courtyard, with a projecting moulded doorway bearing the motto *Pateas Amicis*. This doorway, the Arms of Bishop Graham, from the courtyard gate and a moulded tympanum from a dormer (added to Meil at around the same time) are all preserved in the wall of the kitchen wing which, together with the northern wing, replaced the 1626 house. The Episcopal **Chapel** of St Margaret of Antioch and Scotland was added to the east wing in 1898.

Battery, Breckness, 1940

A concrete tower with projecting roof slabs standing behind an emplacement which housed a twin 6-pounder gun. Other remnants of the camp include two smaller emplacements (each of which held a 12-pounder gun), slit-windowed searchlight positions and a generator house.

21 Greenwall, 1656

The well-preserved house of Patrick Graham of Rothiesholm. Massive walls are pierced by small windows and the plain projecting sandstone door surround enhances its apparent solidity.

St Nicholas Kirk, 1816

Now abandoned; roofed in local slate, with a small bellcote and a weathered sandstone armorial panel set in the session house wall.

In 1615, Bishop George Graham was translated from Dunblane to Orkney. He came north in 1617 to construct houses at **Breckness, Skaill** and **Meil**. His son-in-law, Patrick Smith of Braco, occupied Meil. Two wives and 25 children later, it passed to his fourth son, Patrick, who sold it in turn to his uncle, Patrick Graham of Rothiesholm, second son of the Bishop and then living in **Greenwall**, Holm. Thus Meil became *Graham's Hall*. Later James Graeme changed the spelling of the family name and that of their home. In the 18th and early 19th centuries there were a succession of absentee landlords until the Sutherland Graemes decided to renovate and return to the house, which they retained up until the middle of this century.

Below *Graemeshall*. Middle *Graemeshall: Faith, Hope and Charity*. Bottom *Greenwall*

View of Stromness c.1860, John Irvine

In 1789, James Wright of the Stanley expedition remarked, *I never in my life saw such a singular place. It is very long, consisting of one zigzag street or rather lane extending along the shore, and which in many places in not above 4ft in breadth.* Newly graduated from Georgian Edinburgh, he was not greatly impressed and suggested *If the least attention had been paid to regularity in the formation of this street, the place would have been by no means so despicable, for the houses in general are tolerable, consisting of two stories and covered with fine Blue Slate.*

Stromness waterfront early this century (see p 51)

STROMNESS

Hamnavoe is a long bay, lying on the south-west corner of the Mainland of Orkney. Although it opens into Hoy Sound it is well protected by the granite ridge of Brinkie's Brae which forms its western edge. Huddled along this boundary, and spreading up the Brae, is the town of Stromness.

Little is known of the early history of the town, save a few brief mentions in the Saga. As late as 1642, Stromness consisted of five or six houses and a few thatched huts. By 1794 the hamlet had grown to a sizeable settlement of 222 houses (130 of these having slate roofs). The town's function has always been as a harbour and today it is the main port for transport to the Scottish Mainland by Ro-Ro ferry. The first houses grew up along the water's edge and, as the town expanded, it stretched along the bay and in places up the hill. The houses, built gable on to the sea, belonged to merchants and were accompanied by such outbuildings and piers as were necessary to sustain their commerce. Further houses, built uphill, formed a narrow, winding lane running parallel to the sea. Steep closes ran from the water to what is now the main street and from there up the hill.

In 1758, Stromness won a 15-year legal battle with Kirkwall for the right to trade outwith the restrictive levies which had, until then, been imposed by the Royal Burgh as part of its rights of charter. This opened the way for Stromness to act as a port for local industries, such as kelp and herring, as well as for many varied imports. Sixty years of war in the English Channel between 1688 and 1815 meant that the northern route via Orkney became more attractive to North Sea shipping: especially to vessels *en route* to North America. Stromness's situation made it an ideal port for provisioning vessels and a collecting point for crew and it was frequented by the Royal Navy, by whalers and, in particular, by the Hudson's Bay Company. Increased wheeled traffic in the 19th-century led to the widening of the street, although it remains narrow and twisting.

The **Pierhead** is the modern centre of Stromness although until the late 19th century the only piers would have been those beside individual houses.

The **Warehouse**, *c.*1675, is an exceptionally broad building on two floors with a Caithness slate roof, built for James Gordon of Cairston in an attempt to cash in on the American rice trade.

22 **Stromness Hotel**, 1901
A bulky L-shaped block that presents a narrow symmetrical frontage to the street, topped by former gables and tiny bartizans. In the Second World War it served as OS Def HQ, the Army's Orkney and Shetland Defence Headquarters, and Gracie Fields sang from its balcony. To the north, the main street continues on to **John Street** with the **Town House** and **Masonic Hall**, 1889, in similar plain and workmanlike Jacobean.

23 **Millar's House**, 13 John Street, 17th century
A solid pedimented sandstone door surround bearing the arms of Millar and Nesbet fronts a two-storey house standing at the head of a flight of steps. It was home to Lt James Millar RN, who led a distinguished naval career in the early 19th century.

Speedings, 40 John Street, early 19th century
A three-storey house with dormered attic, dominating the north end of Stromness, it was

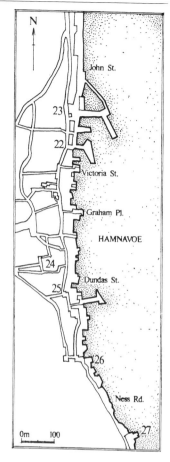

Left *Speedings*. Below *Millar's House*

The old Parish Kirk in June 1963

Walter Scott in 1814 was not impressed: *Stromness is a little dirty straggling town, which cannot be traversed by a cart, or even by a horse, for there are stairs up and down, even in the principal streets. We paraded its whole length like turkeys in a string, I suppose to satisfy ourselves that there was a worse town in the Orkneys than the metropolis, Kirkwall.* This, however, was to miss the point, since the main thoroughfare of Stromness was the sheltered water of Hamnavoe.

Right *Pier Arts Centre*
Below *Off Leslie's Close*

Alexander Graham was the leader of a group of Stromness merchants who fought a protracted legal battle against Kirkwall from 1743 onwards over an anomaly in the Act of Union which, despite allowing *all the subjects ... full freedom ... of trade*, gave Royal Burghs leave to levy onerous taxes on traders outside their boundaries. Their case was upheld in 1758 but the legal costs ruined Graham who ended up in prison for his debts. However, it is largely thanks to him that Stromness grew into a major 18th- and 19th-century trading post.

built by Lt James Robertson RN, who commanded HMS *Beresford* at the Battle of Plattsburg in 1812, and hence became known as the Lieutenant's House.

Primary School, 1967, A T Jamieson, County Architect
A bold rectilinear composition. Uncompromising modernism with a white window grid and red gables. Its dominating bulk looks ill at ease with the small scale, *ad hoc* townscape, though the occasional glimpse of the contrast is striking.

Pier Arts Centre, early 19th century, (see p 51) renovated 1978, Kate Heron with Levitt Bernstein Associates
The house, warehouse and pier of Edward Clouston, Hudson's Bay Company agent from 1836 to 1867. Now converted into an award-winning gallery with its own permanent collection. The layout and character of the two-and-a-half-storey house has been largely retained, notably the white panelled drawing room which now functions as a library. The stone-built warehouse has been converted into a particularly fine gallery space.

Community Centre, Church Road, 1814
The former parish church, standing at the head of Church Road, shorn of its original pyramid spire.

St Mary's Episcopal Church, Church Road, late 19th century
Tall lancet windows give it the appearance of a church, but the side walls betray the domestic origins of the Episcopal mission in a dwellinghouse.

Further south, the main street opens out into **Graham Place**. Alexander Graham's 19th-century two-storey house lies along its eastern side with a narrow garden fronting the street.

24 **Leslie's Close** leads up the hill, lined with two-storey houses. A pleasant garden courtyard opens off it, enclosed by two 19th-century houses with brightly painted woodwork. Opposite, a steep stone-paved lane rises to a picturesque grouping of gables, roofs and the protruding rock of Brinkie's Brae. From here, the **Khyber Pass**, Stromness' quintessential close, descends between high walls and corbelled corners to the main street. **Franklin Road** continues south along the brae, with views over flagstoned roofs to the harbour and beyond, until meeting the equally picturesque **Puffer's Close** which descends as steep stone-paved slopes and winding steps into Dundas Street.

Dundas Street is narrow and picturesque with many intruding gables, such as that of **No 42,** home of Eliza Fraser whose adventures as a castaway in Australia inspired Patrick White's novel *A Fringe of Leaves*.

Lifeboat Station, Dundas Street, 1925
There has been a lifeboat at Stromness since 1867, first based at a slipway at Ness, then moored in the harbour until this geometric, barrel-roofed, red-oxide painted shed was built.

25 **Melvin Place**, set amid 18th-century houses, contains a narrow square-plan house with garden whose trees soften and broaden out the street to form an attractive and sunny square. The evocatively named **Hellihole Road** climbs from here up the hillside. South from Melvin Place, the street winds on as **Alfred Street**.

T Kent - Orkney Library

RCAHMS

Top *Dundas Street looking towards Graham Place around the turn of the century*. Above *Gable of 84 Dundas Street – Melvin Place in 1963*. Bottom left *15 and 17 Alfred Street*

Burgher

Youth Hostel, Hellihole Road, 1888, T S Peace
Built as the Volunteers' Drill Hall, and bearing all the hallmarks of Peace's oeuvre: dressed

The Hudson's Bay Company, founded in 1670, found the Orcadians to be *more sober and tractable than the Irish, and they engage for lower wages than either the English or the Irish*. As a result, around three-quarters of those employed in their settlements were said to be of Orcadian extraction. With annual wages of £20-30 for tradesmen and £6-18 for labourers (at a time when a schoolmaster in Stromness could expect to earn £8.00) many young men left the farms to exploit this trade. This left a shortage of farm workers but many settled in Canada or returned to build houses in Stromness.

Stromness Museum

George Mackay Brown, born in Stromness in 1921, studied for a year at Newbattle Abbey College when Edwin Muir was its warden, and gained a degree in English from Edinburgh University. Brown's work includes *Selected Poems*, the novels *Magnus* and *Greenvoe* and the vivid, personal introductions to the islands: *An Orkney Tapestry* and *Portrait of Orkney*. From here he writes 'Under Brinkie's Brae', a weekly column in the local newspaper, the *Orcadian*.

Lighthouse Shore Station

stone walls, slate roof with projecting joist ends and large arched doorways, set under gablets.

White House, Whitehouse Lane, 1680
Supposedly the first house in Stromness to be constructed with lime mortar (hence the name). It was the home of the Stewarts of Massetter, who played host to Captain Bligh in 1780 on his visit with Cook's ships. George Stewart served on the *Bounty* during the 1789 mutiny and provided the model for Byron's 'Torquil'.

Haven, Alfred Street, 18th century
The home of Hudson's Bay Company agents from 1771 to 1836. The modern pier and sheds are the base from which the mv *Pole Star* services the lighthouses and navigation buoys of the North of Scotland.

26 **Stromness Museum**, 1858
A curious blend of irregular Stromness planning and sub-classical pilaster framing, the two-storey former Town Hall houses the collection of Orkney Natural History Society which was founded in 1937. It now includes exhibits on the history of Stromness and Scapa Flow as well as Orkney's wildlife. *Open to the public*

10 and **12 South End**, 18th century
With a double gable to the street, the former Login's Inn has two floors and an attic, while a low addition on its pier features Gothic-style windows. In the 1830s this had *the just credit of being one of the most comfortable inns in the North of Scotland*. The well across the street was the watering place of the ships of the Hudson's Bay Company and of Captain Cook's and Franklin's expeditions.

Lighthouse Shore Station, Ness Road, 1892
Victorian 'lego-brick' accommodation for the families of Sule Skerry lightkeepers. White-painted with black trim, its door is protected by a heavy wooden canopy on stout posts, while over the door a relief panel depicts a lighthouse.

27 **Double Houses**, Ness Road, early 19th century
The last Stromness houses to push their gables out on to piers on the seawards side of the road: a long, double two-storey row.

Stenigar, Ness Road, 1836, converted 1948, Stanley Cursiter with Robertson & Hendry
This long two-storey block with local stone walls

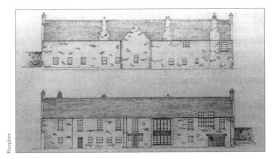

Burgher

Stenigar, Stromness, by Robertson and Hendry in possession of Mrs Thomas

and roof was originally the hub of John Stanger's boatyard. In 1856 the paddle-steamer *Royal Mail* was built here. After fitting out on the Tyne, it went on to establish the first regular Pentland Firth crossing. The yard closed in 1926 and, after war service as a recreation centre, it became the comfortable house of artist Stanley Cursiter. The wooden external stair was brought inside, timber boarding came from an old army hut, 18th-century doors from Kirknewton and the double doors, which link the high studio to the barrel-vaulted living room, from an Edinburgh flat. Externally, the two-storey bow window to living and dining rooms and the small windows round the door are reminiscent of Mackintosh's domestic architecture. Wall and roof windows light the studio and give a view along the shore of the town.

Ness Battery, 1938

Guarding the western entrance to Scapa Flow in the Second World War were massive 6-in. guns whose two large emplacements still stand, given an improvised roof of concrete carried on a network of steel beams to protect the gunners

Stanley Cursiter (1887-1976) was born in Kirkwall and went to Edinburgh, becoming an assistant in a printing firm after abandoning hopes of becoming an architect. Through evening classes and then full-time study at Edinburgh College of Art he gained a scholarship to the Royal College of Art, London, where he studied under Lethaby before returning to Edinburgh. In 1930 he became Director of the National Gallery of Scotland and His Majesty's Limner in Scotland, producing paintings of state occasions. He maintained his interest in architecture, redesigning the interior of the National Gallery of Scotland and, in 1928, drew up unrealised plans for a new arts centre incorporating a gallery of modern art and an historical collection of Scottish paintings. In painting he experimented in the style of the Futurists and painted many portraits, but it is for his depictions of St Magnus Cathedral and Orkney's sea and landscapes, that he is best remembered.

The Point of Ness was the centre for the Stromness herring fishing boom from 1893 when wooden jetties and curing stations grew up along its shore: long wooden huts to accommodate as many as 4000-5000 people working on boats or as gutters and packers. By the outbreak of the First World War, however, the importance of Stromness as a herring port had ended.

Fishing boats leaving Stromness, 1906

T Kent - Orkney Library

from air attack by 1941. Behind them stands a two-storey observation tower and from here all the western defences of the Flow were controlled. Along the shore are the remains of a later, separate, twin 6-pounder battery and searchlight emplacements.

Stromness Academy, 1982-9, Orkney Islands Architects: M M Gilbertson, R G Dewar & J Lee
The new Stromness Secondary School is broken down into a series of teaching blocks arranged loosely around a courtyard. A bright glass-roofed entrance hall leads into a comfortable interior, which manages to avoid long dimly lit corridors and to create a variety of attractive spaces – notably a timber-lined library on two levels.

Quildon Cottage, Back Road, 19th century
An attractive conversion of former traditional farm buildings in local stone, stepped up from the road and with a round grain-drying kiln.

Oglaby, Outertown Road, 1894
A well-proportioned Baronial villa, L-plan with the usual collection of crowstepped gables and a steep-roofed turret.

28 **Breckness**, 1633 (see p 50)
The solid two-storey house of Bishop George Graham, now ruined, was built on an L-plan. The door, unusually, is placed on the outside of the L. Its moulded jambs remain but the Bishop's armorial panel which surmounted it has been removed to Skaill. A straight flight of stairs rose directly inside the door with the kitchen, and large arched fireplace to the right. From this remote but beautiful corner of the island the Breckness Estate extended over a large part of the West Mainland.

WEST MAINLAND: SANDWICK
Sandwick lies on the west coast of the Mainland, north of Stromness and consists mainly of a broad valley, tapering from the northern ends of the Lochs of Harray and Stenness to the Bay of Skaill with the cliffs at Yesnaby and the precariously balanced stack known as the 'Castle' lying to the south and the 129m Vestra Field, or 'Western Hill', to the north.

Top Oglaby. *Middle* Kitchen *fireplace, Breckness (see p 51). Above* Mill of Rango

29 **Mill of Rango**, 19th century (kiln 1895)
A pyramid-roofed kiln and a dormered upper doorway reached by a bridge arching over the

mill lade add interest to the normally stark rectangular form of an Orkney mill. The Breckness Estate had a mill on the site from the 17th century and the building immediately to the west of the present mill is probably an older one. The present owner is restoring the building and mill.

West Aith

West Aith, 19th century
A long low crofting range of traditional Orkney construction; with thatch covering to the main roofs of house and outbuildings and bare flags on the porch added in front of its south-facing door.

Skaill House, early 17th century
Orkney's finest ancient mansion. Built for Bishop George Graham and begun as a plain two-storey block opening on to a courtyard to

Skaill, west elevation

the south. This was later expanded by the addition of a second parallel block to the south and an L-shaped wing of offices to the north: itself lengthened and carried out to the east in the 19th and early 20th centuries. The result is a long and varied western elevation with a screen wall which links its various elements to shelter a small garden court. The newer north wing has taller crowstepped corner blocks, a narrow linking passage with windows on either side, and rows of pedimented dormers overlooking a walled garden. The landscaped grounds include an 18th-century shed-roofed doocot. The plain white **Kierfiold**, 1750, was the dower house.

30 **Skara Brae**, Bay of Skaill, *c.*3000-2500BC
The long white curve of the Bay of Skaill breaks the western line of cliffs to open into the Atlantic and may have been formed by the erosion of a freshwater loch, on whose shores stood the farming and fishing community of Skara Brae. Its houses are stone walled, roughly square in plan and built into earlier

Skara Brae, Sandwick (see p 51)

middens with narrow paved linking passages and low doorways. The spacious houses which stand to wall-head level have central hearths and would have been roofed by skin or turf carried on wooden or whalebone rafters. The most notable feature of the houses, however, is their furniture; with flagstones used to construct dressers with shelves and vertical divisions and beds which would have been lined with heather. In the floor, small tanks have been made of flagstone sealed with clay; perhaps to store shellfish for bait. Small chambers open off most of the huts, some next to the doors to allow them to be barred and some with stone-lined drains which may well have been lavatories several millenniums before the Romans arrived in the south of Britain. At one end of the main passage is a small, paved open court and, next to it, a building without beds which has been identified as a workshop.
Open to the public: guidebook available

Thorfinn the Mighty was Earl of Orkney from 1014 until around 1065 and was the greatest of Orkney's Viking rulers. The son of Earl Sigurd II of Orkney and of a daughter of King Malcolm II of Scotland, his rule expanded to nine Scottish Earldoms and may have reached as far as Fife. Despite Shakespeare's version of events, it seems likely that Thorfinn joined with Macbeth to oust Duncan and that this joint rule of Scotland was reached by agreement as a long period of relative peace ensued. Thorfinn went on a pilgrimage to the Holy Land and on his return to Birsay built *a fine minster there, the seat of the first Bishop of Orkney.*

St Peter's Church, Skaill, 1836 (see p 52)
The cramped well-preserved interior of this small, plain church is dominated by its towering pulpit. Set against the southern wall, it is flanked by a pair of tall, arched windows and would have put the preacher on a level with those of his parishioners in the U-shaped gallery an effect, calculated or otherwise, to strike the fear of God into those below.

Quoyloo Church, 19th century (see p 52)
The most vividly decorated Presbyterian church in Orkney; its colour scheme is based on proposals by the artist Stanley Cursiter and includes sky-blue pews, red carpets and dado

and pale yellow walls. Despite using all three primary colours, the result is surprisingly harmonious, if a little unusual.

BIRSAY (see p 52)

Making up the north-western corner of the Mainland, Birsay stretches from the green and low-lying land around the Brough of Birsay across the Lochs of Boardhouse and Hundland to the bleak moorland north-east of Dounby. Birsay was the seat of Norse power when Kirkwall was little more than a village, with both Bishops and Earls holding sway from here.

Twatt Airfield, 1940-4

As Second World War Fleet Air Arm base HMS *Tern*, Twatt was home to some twenty different types of aircraft including Seafires and Hurricanes. The extensive remains of brick and concrete airfield buildings include the **control tower** which rises over a bunker protected by earth embankments. The **cinema**, though less elaborate than that on Hoy, still contains a concrete ticket desk, projection windows, and stage, the boards of which were trod by such stars of ENSA shows as Gracie Fields.

Twatt Kirk, 1874

A tall stone church, the interior features a rich colour scheme by the artist Stanley Cursiter: deep burgundy pews, green carpets, brown painted gallery and a sky-blue screen with gold stars behind the pulpit.

Kitchener Memorial, Marwick Head, 1924

A square squat tower atop 80m cliffs, built to commemorate the loss of the 11,000-ton British cruiser HMS *Hampshire*, with all but 12 of its crew, on 5 June 1916. It struck a mine *en route* to Russia with the Minister of War, Lord Kitchener, on board.

31 Boardhouse Mill, 1873

The only working watermill in Orkney, with an overshot wheel. The previous meal mill, a much smaller building with an undershot wheel is sited downstream, to the east of a large farm steading built round a courtyard which also features a large waterwheel to drive threshing machinery. In the early 17th century Orkney had more than 50 watermills, probably all of the vertical type. Most of those which can be seen today are 19th-century extensions or replacements of these.

Below *Control tower, Twatt.* Middle *Boardhouse mill stones, 1968*

Boardhouse Mill to the left with the old Barony Mill and Threshing Mill

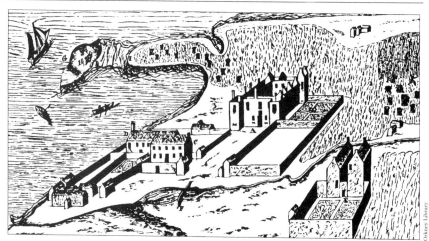

Earl's Palace drawn by George Low 1774

John Brand in 1701 noted that the upper floor of the palace *hath been prettily decorated, the ceiling being all painted, and that for the most part with schems holding forth scripture histories of Noah's flood, Christ's riding to Jerusalem etc. And the scripture is set down beside the figure. It was inhabited within these twenty years but is now fast decaying.*

St Magnus Kirk

Earl's Palace, Birsay, *c.*1574 (see p 52)
The crumbling ruin of Earl Robert Stewart's palace retains enough of its grandeur to indicate that it was indeed *a sumptuous and stately building.* Built round a courtyard with a well, it has two tall storeys with towers at three corners. The entrance was under a 'gallery' in the south wing, while the slightly later northern wing contained the kitchen, remnants of whose great fireplace and chimney can still be seen. Contemporary drawings show that upper windows on the north and east were part dormered and pedimented and that the palace was surrounded by flower and herb gardens, rabbit warrens, a bowling green and archery butts. Seventeenth-century drawings of the palace record a two-arched **Bridge** on axis with the palace gate, corresponding with the lower section of the present 1872 structure. *Open to the public*

St Magnus Kirk, Birsay, 1760
Standing just outside the palace precinct this long single-storey church replaced the cruciform Christ's Kirk built by Earl Thorfinn after his pilgrimage to Rome, *c.*1050. The Revd George Low's drawing of 1771 shows the church as having two floors with an external stair at the west end. Fragments of older buildings incorporated within the present arrangement include a 17th-century belfry and a lancet window sill bearing the word *Bellus; Mons Bellus* being the name given to the medieval palace of the Bishops of Orkney in the 16th century whose foundations may well lie under this site.

32 The **Brough of Birsay**, a wedge-shaped tidal
island lying to the north, contains the remains
of a Norse settlement, including the ruin of the
12th-century **St Peter's Church**. The
rectangular nave is lined with stone benches
and has two semicircular recesses for side
altars sited in front of the chancel arch. The
chancel, containing a red sandstone altar
reconstructed during excavation, ends in a
round apse which may have been vaulted. To
the east, 12th-century Norse house foundations
overlie previous periods of occupation. Other
longhouse foundations lie further up the hill
and a Pictish well and symbol stone have been
located on the site. *Open to visitors (tide
permitting): guidebook available*

Lighthouse, Brough of Birsay, 1925
An unmanned lighthouse on a low round
castellated tower joined to a cubic gas store.

Sule Skerry Lighthouse, 1891-4
The desolate 35-acre island of Sule Skerry lies
60km to the west of Brough Head with the
steep outcrop of Stack Skerry 6km beyond it.
Topped by an especially large glazed lantern
the straight-sided 27m brick tower afforded
accommodation for the keepers whose families
were housed in Stromness. As the most remote
lighthouse in the British Isles its only contact
with the outside world (between visits of the
mv *Pole Star*) was provided by carrier pigeon.

33 **Kirbister Farm**, 1723, restoration 1987,
Orkney Islands Council
Though now preserved as a representative
example of an old Orkney farmhouse, this was a
much larger than average dwelling with walls
reaching 2.5m in height rather than the more
usual 1.8m. The date of the house is recorded on
a door lintel and the main room of the house is
the 'firehouse', formerly the kitchen or 'but' end.
The hearth is built against a low stone wall, the
'fire back', in the centre of the room and vents
through a wooden 'smoke hole' in the ridge,
which normally provided light as well. Venting
was assisted by moving the top board, attached
to a pole, according to the wind direction. The
thickness of the wall contains a neuk bed and
flagstone-shelved recesses for storage purposes.
The outbuildings include a barn with a circular
grain-drying kiln, a pigsty and a smith's forge.
Open to the public: guidebook available

Above *St Peter's Church.*
Below *Sule Skerry Lighthouse.*
Bottom *Kirbister Farm 'firehouse'*

Click Mill, Birsay.

Click Mill, Mill Brig, *c.*1823, J Spence
The only Orkney example of a horizontal watermill, a type common in Shetland where the steeper topography gave watercourses the power to turn a small set of horizontally mounted millstones by means of a small wooden wheel or 'tirl' connected directly to the upper stone. Orkney was more suited to the larger vertical mills which served a whole estate or district. *Open to the public: leaflet available*

34 **DOUNBY**
Dounby is a relatively modern hamlet which has grown up since the 19th century at the meeting point of the parishes of Sandwick, Birsay and Harray and the crossing of roads from Birsay to Kirkwall and Stromness to Evie. It became an important market place with market green and shops beside the crossroads and is still the location for the annual West Mainland Agricultural Show.

U F Church, Dounby, 1947
A cruciform church entered by an elliptical arch-headed door with a splayed surround.

HARRAY
Harray, originally linked to Birsay, is Orkney's only inland parish and slopes down from hills in the east to a fertile plain beside the Loch of Harray.

Below *Holodyke, Harray.*
Bottom *Merkister, Harray*

35 **Holodyke**, 1888, altered 1896, Reginald Fairlie
The original two-storey block has been expanded with the addition of a steeply pitched roofed north wing and entrance tower. Holodyke was built for Sir Thomas Smith Clouston, 1840-1915, youngest son of Robert Clouston of nearby Nisthouse, superintendent of Edinburgh's Morningside Asylum and author of *An Asylum or Hospital Home with Plans.*

Merkister Hotel, 1910; altered
Built for Robert Linklater and changed from Ingleneuk to Merkister in 1934 by his writer son, Eric. Recent extensions have accompanied its transformation into a hotel.

Harray Mill, 1876
A two-storey stone building with a neatly arched doorway and a tall stair window; the kiln has an unusual ventilator which runs the length of its ridge.

Eric Linklater (1899-1974) though born in Penarth, Glamorganshire, always identified himself with his father's home. One of Scotland's most eminent 20th-century men of letters, he achieved fame through the success of his novel *Juan in America* (1931) and a string of other popular novels including *Magnus Merriman* (1934), *Private Angelo* (1946), *The Dark of Summer* (1956) and *Position at Noon* (1958). He was also responsible for a series of non-fiction works including three volumes of autobiography. He is buried in Harray churchyard.

Bridge, Scuan, 17th century
Spanning the burn of Corrigal and constructed
in halves: upstream with flagstones and
downstream with two low semicircular arches.
A stone in the upstream side bears the
inscription IL 1694 and two carved faces.

36 **Corrigal Farm Museum**, (see p 69)
Midhouse of Corrigal, 18th/19th century;
restoration 1980, Orkney Islands Council
The house at Corrigal is much later than its
counterpart at Kirbister. The open fire back has
become incorporated in a cross wall which
divides the but-end into an area oot-bye the fire
(used for tasks such as grinding grain or
making butter) and an in-bye or kitchen/living
area. The outbuildings are separated from the
house by a narrow 'kloss' and include a byre
with upright flagstone divisions and a stone-
lined central drain. The barn has stables and a
typical beehive-shaped kiln for drying grain,
heated by smoke and air from a peat fire, led
through a low tunnel at ground level. These
were a common feature of Orkney steadings
prior to the construction of large-scale kilns in
the late 19th century. Corrigal, occupied until
well into this century, is now an APRS and
Civic Trust award-winning museum which
houses a wide variety of farming and domestic
artefacts. *Open to the public: guidebook
available*

Top *Corrigal*. Above *Kiln, Corrigal*.

St Michael's Kirk, 1836
A plain white rendered church with Caithness
slate roof and semicircular arched windows.
From its hilltop vantage point it overlooks its
Free Church rival, built in 1844 and expanded
30 years later. **St Michael's Manse**, 1856, is a
five-bay house, built for the Revd Samuel Traill,
incorporating a tall moulded doorcase and
piended, octagonal attic dormers.

37 **Holland House**, Harray, 1844
Built for the Free Kirk opposite, and a
particularly fine example of a pattern of manse
seen throughout Orkney; three-bay, two-storey,
with a central hallway and stair, a gently
sloping piended roof and central chimneys.
Dunsyre, 19th century, is a large villa, similar
in form but with a bay window in the end wall
and an elegant Ionic-columned door surround.

St Michael's Manse

Winksetter, 16th century or older
A long croft house which may have had Norse

Top *Dunsyre, Harray*. Middle *Winksetter, Harray*. Above *Tormiston Mill, Stenness*. Below *Maeshowe*

origins: it has outbuildings across a narrow close which contain a neuk bed. The house contains a quern-ledder, a projecting shelf to carry a quern stone and the fire back has had a cross wall built around it and, later, a small fireplace built inside the original one.

STENNESS

Stenness lies on the north side of the Orphir range of hills and slopes down to the Lochs of Harray and Stenness.

Tormiston Mill, *c.*1885

A well-preserved three-storey meal mill. Its conversion into a restaurant and shop won a European Architectural Heritage Award in 1975. The original machinery, although somewhat obscured by this process, is still mostly intact. *Open to the public*

38 Maeshowe, *c.*2750 BC

Europe's finest prehistoric tomb has a tall central chamber at the heart of a large green mound, entered by a low passageway with three small side chambers opening off it. The most notable feature apart from its size is the quality of its construction in massive slabs of flagstone. Four vertical slabs support corner buttresses in the square central chamber which corbels inwards. One wall of the entrance passage and the roofs of the cells are formed by immense single stones. On the winter solstice the sun sets over the Hoy Hills, and shines directly up the passageway on to the back wall of the tomb. *Open to the public: guidebook available*

St Magnus Cathedral: Top *Spire.*
Left *From the south-east.* Middle
Nave. Above *South Transept*

49

Top *Bishop's Palace, Kirkwall.*
Middle *Cromwell Road, Kirkwall.*
Above *Breckness with St John's
Head, Hoy.* Top right *Albert Street,
Kirkwall: 'the Tree' as it looked until
recently.* Right *Tankerness House,
Kirkwall.*

Top *Stromness waterfront.*
Left *Pier Arts Centre, Stromness.*
Middle *Breckness, kitchen fireplace.*
Above *Skara Brae*

51

Burgher

Burgher

Burgher

Burgher

Burgher

On Christmas Day 1814 it was discovered that a tenant farmer, Captain MacKay, tired of the invasion by curious visitors, had begun to demolish the Stones of Stenness. By the time he was stopped, he had already broken up the 'Stone of Odin', a monolith with a hole through it which Scott had suggested might have been used in sacrifices to *'bind a victim'*. As Hossack observed, this tradition was continued, though not quite literally, by lovers who would 'plight their troth' by clasping hands through the hole. Divorce was equally easily achieved; the couple would part within the former Stenness Church and leave by opposite doors. This church stood on the site of the present 1910 building and had a semi-circular tower.

Left *Stones of Stenness.*
Below *Stenness by George Low*

Stones of Stenness, *c.*2500 BC (see p 71)

Only four stones of an original circle of twelve survive and their rock-cut ditch is partly obscured, but their height (the tallest is over 5m) still makes this an impressive monument. The 6.5m menhir known as the **Watch Stone** which guards the causeway is also associated with the ring.

39 Ring of Brodgar, *c.*2500 BC

A wide circle of standing stones on the opposite promontory from the Watch Stone. Twenty-seven still stand, while four lie prone and stumps of nine others are visible; originally there may have been as many as sixty. The tallest is 5.6m high, and the whole monument is surrounded by a deep ditch. There are outlying barrows and monoliths, including the Comet Stone to the south-west.

Opposite: Top *Earl's Palace, Birsay: the courtyard.* Middle left *St Peter's Church, Skaill.* Below left *Earl's Palace, Birsay: window.* Right *Quoyloo Kirk with Stanley Cursiter's colour scheme.* Bottom *Birsay, seascape*

Ring of Brodgar

Above right *Mill of Eyrland.* Below *Hall of Clestrain. Tentative reconstruction by Simpson & Brown*

Simpson & Brown

Unstan Cairn, 3500-3000 BC

A long communal tomb with a small side chamber and upright flagstone divisions, a form unique to Orkney and developed in full at Rousay. The side chamber lintel incorporates a Viking runic inscription and carving of a bird. *Open to the public*

Brig o' Waithe, 1859

A substantial structure with three segmental arches which crosses the tidal strait between the Loch of Stenness and the sea.

40 Mill of Eyrland, c.1862

A three-storey mill built on an L-plan with a kiln on the corner, the mill in one wing and a house in the other. Now sensitively converted into a private house.

Burgher

ORPHIR

Orphir lies along the northern edge of Scapa Flow, rising from a steep shoreline to the ridge of hills which divides it from Stenness in the north, reaching 270m at Mid Hill, the highest point on the Mainland. At its heart lies the 2km long Loch of Kirbister.

41 Hall of Clestrain, 1769

The original house, attacked and looted in 1725 by the pirate John Gow, was replaced for Patrick Honyman by the present elegant Georgian mansion, whose broad projecting centre bay was probably topped by a shallow pediment.

42 St Nicholas Kirk, c.1120

Only the semicircular apse still stands, the circular nave having been demolished in 1757 to provide stone for the adjacent parish church, now itself gone. The building is thought to have

Clare Hammond

The *Orkneyinga Saga* describes the layout of the Earl's Bu in some detail: there was a *'door in the south wall near the eastern gable, and in front of the hall, just a few paces down from it, stood a fine church. On the left as you came into the hall was a large stone slab with a lot of big ale vats behind it and opposite the door was the living room* from which Svein Asleifarson escaped through a skylight.

Left *St Nicholas Kirk.*
Below *Earl's Bu and Kirk*

RCAHMS

been inspired by a visit to the Church of the Holy Sepulchre in Jerusalem by Earl Hakon Paulsson, earlier responsible for the killing of St Magnus on Egilsay. Nearby are the low grass topped foundation of his drinking hall (**Bu** in Old Norse).

Gyre, 1886
Gyre was purchased by William Halcro of Coubister in 1737 and is still inhabited by his descendants. A house was built in *c.*1795 with an earlier wing to the east. The two-storey harled extension to the west was added in 1851. This first house was replaced in 1886 by the present dressed stone block with a broad asymmetrical gable to the south and a castellated tower to the north.

Orphir Church, 1885
A former United Free Church, with round-headed windows and a gallery to the west. A tall and pointed ridge ventilator acts as a mini-spire.

Swanbister House, *c.*1846, altered early 20th century
A three-bay house with octagonal attic dormers, a freestone porch and a lower eastern wing with

Gyre

Burgher

Top *Swanbister, Orphir.*
Above *Smoogro, Orphir.*

gabled dormers. It was built by Archer Fortescue, *a Devonshire gentleman* who bought and improved the estate, and alarmed the natives by bringing with him *a first-rate pack of hunting harriers.*

Smoogro House, 17th century, altered
The original two-storey block was built probably for one Thomas Sinclair, fined £80 in 1677 for 'ryving' his neighbours' hair, hurling them 'furth of their chairs' and even running them through with swords. A parallel block was added in the early 19th century and later, in 1903, given a steeply pitched attic floor with high flagstone-topped crowsteps and moulded dormers. At this time it was owned by Sir Thomas Clouston and closely resembles work done for him at **Holodyke** by Reginald Fairlie.

Kirbister Meal Mill, 1889
An extensive two-and-a-half-storey mill complex originally provided with two kilns and two waterwheels, one for grain milling and one for threshing. The site was formerly that of a 'Wauk Mill', giving its name to the long sandy bay below.

FIRTH
The parish of Firth curves around the broad bay which gives it its name. The Vikings knew it as 'Aurridafiord' (salmon-trout firth) and it was for many years known for the quality of its oysters.

Earth House, Rennibister Farm, *c.*500 BC
The roughly hexagonal chamber of this underground food store was reached originally by a low passage, now lying under the road. Its corbelled roof, like that at Grain near Kirkwall, was supported on four columns and a series of lintels formed by long round-edged stones. *Open to the public*

Old Firth Manse, 1811
A crowstepped two-and-a-half-storey, three-bay house with pedimented dormers, added to later in the 19th century to form an elegant L-plan residence.

Chambered Cairn, Cuween Hill, *c.*2500 BC
A communal tomb with a low passage leading to a rectangular central chamber (in which were found twenty-four dog skulls) and four side chambers, all 2m in height. *Open to the public*

Old Firth Manse

Finstown

43 **FINSTOWN**

Finstown owes its name and its growth as a
settlement to a retired Irish soldier named
'Phin' who established an ale house called the
Toddy Hole in 1822 on the site of the later 19th-
century **Pomona Inn**, a two-storey harled
block with a local slate roof. This was the
junction of the Kirkwall to Stromness road and
the old road to Evie, Rendall and the West
Mainland.

Below *'Boat House' Finstown.*
Middle *Millquoy Mill.* Bottom
Binscarth

Boat House, 1970s
A small holiday chalet, with a roof formed by a
disused mould for fibreglass boats. This
continues an old Orkney tradition of using old
boats to form buildings – usually outhouses.

Meal Mill, Millquoy, 19th century
An L-shaped two-storey block roofed in local
slate. The wing with its gable to the burn made
up the original mill, the taller drying kiln with
its square wooden ventilator having been added
later.

Binscarth House, 1850
A two-storey rendered house with ashlar Tudor
detailing and large bay windows built for
Robert Scarth who, as a bank agent, acted as
factor to many of the larger estates in Orkney.
Binscarth Farm, c.1845, has a large stone-
built farm steading with distinctive pyramid
roofs arranged around a courtyard that has
been roofed over during the present century.

44 **Langalour**, Redland Farm, 18th century
A ruined crofthouse, whose south-facing door

Langalour, showing neuk bed

Below *Breck of Rendall.*
Bottom *Doocot*

leads into a former fire hoose. This has been divided by a cross wall into an in-bye with a pair of neuk beds; and an oot-bye with a quern-ledder.

Estabin was the home of **John Firth**, whose *Reminiscences of an Orkney Parish* is the definitive work on the organisation of the old Orkney croft.

RENDALL
Rendall is a small parish on the north-east corner of the West Mainland, linked to its neighbour Evie.

Mossetter, late 18th century
The ruined crofthouse of Mossetter demonstrates clearly the typical shared doorway of house and byre. It has a long row of nest-holes by the fire and a crosswall has been built over its originally open fire. Its most unusual feature, however, is a long outshot which runs the length of the original fire hoose which contains in-bye two neuk beds with their corbelled roof support by an upright flagstone, and oot-bye, a stone dresser which closely resembles those at Skara Brae.

Breck of Rendall, 19th century
A particularly large and impressive stone-built farm steading, whose two floors and row of arched sheds are ranged around a courtyard. The attractive, traditional rendered house opposite is older, with two floors above the road and another at the level of the garden.

45 **Doocot**, Hall of Rendall, 17th century
A beehive-shaped structure in local stone, it has projecting courses of thin flagstone designed to prevent rats from climbing and getting into it. Inside, gaps in the masonry provide nest-holes for the pigeons.

EVIE
Forming a linked parish with Rendall, Evie makes up a narrow green strip sloping down from the central range of hills to the tumultuous waters of Eynhallow Sound.

Woodwick House, 1912 and earlier
Around 1560 the church lands of Our Lady of Woodwick passed to the Murrays who held it for three generations until it came into the hands of one David McLellan. He was probably the builder of the house shown on Murdo Mackenzie's charts in 1750 as well as the lean-

to roofed **doocot** beside the burn. This structure bears McLellan's arms and is dated 1648. The estate passed to the Traills around 1700 in whose hands it remained until after the house took its present well-proportioned two-storey form. With a tower over the door, a castellated conservatory and crowsteps, it makes a late and somewhat half-hearted attempt at Baronial revival.

Evie School, 1978, Orkney Islands Council Architects: M M Gilbertson
An open-plan school successfully disguising its deep-plan classrooms behind a series of low cupboard outshots which break up its long eaves line and reduce its scale.

Woodwick

46 **Broch of Gurness**, *c.*100 BC and later
Of around 500 brochs known to exist, over a fifth are in Orkney. One of the best preserved is at Gurness, its round tower surrounded by the extensive remains of an encircling village with a defensive outer ditch and ramparts. The tower, which stands to a height of around 2.5m, has passages and cells within its walls and contains internal divisions of stone and flagstone and a well cut into the rock beneath. Around it has grown up a slightly later village with a 'street' which leads up to the low door of the broch and encircles it. The houses which open off it then back on to the deep ditch and show an extraordinary range of constructional techniques using local stone in all its forms. They were lit by small stone lamps with rounded stone circular depressions in them. These can be seen all over the site. A Pictish

Below and bottom Broch of Gurness (see p 69)

3MW Wind Generator, Burgar (see p 69)

Houton Seaplane Base, Orphir in First World War

house, with five small rounded cells opening off a central chamber with a hearth, has been moved from the village site to near the gate. *Open to the public: leaflet available.*

47 **Wind Energy Site**, Burgar Hill, 1980-7
A group of three wind generators which have pioneered the harnessing of this renewable energy source. The first two were the 20m diameter two-bladed rotor of the Wind Energy Group's machine and the more elegant three-bladed Howden HWP 300. Its slender steel tower, hinged at the base, has earned it a number of design awards. In 1987 they were joined by a 3MW Wind Energy Group generator, its cylindrical tower 45m in height to the rotor centre. Its twin-bladed rotor is 60m across. All three now feed electricity to the National Grid.

SOUTH ISLES and SCAPA FLOW
To the south of the Mainland lies a broad expanse of water with islands strung around it like a necklace. With openings to the south, west and formerly to the east, Scapa Flow has a long history as a secure haven, accessible in all weathers: providing a refuge for 18th- and 19th-century sailing ships rounding the North of Scotland and today providing a deep-water berth for oil tankers. However, it was in two World Wars that Scapa Flow achieved fame (and notoriety) and once again put Orkney at the centre of European history. As the main British anchorage in both wars, it drew to the

islands a naval and military population which
greatly outnumbered its civilian one and its
defences left their mark throughout the islands
in brick and concrete: in gun batteries, camps
and airfields. However, it also led to the linking
of the eastern islands in an engineering project
inconceivable in peacetime and left Orkney with
a continuing reminder of the better side of
human nature in the Italian Chapel.

Churchill Barriers, 1940-4, (see p 69)
Sir Arthur Whitaker
In the First World War, the eastern approaches
to the Flow had been rendered un-navigable by
the sinking of old merchant ships in each
channel. However, in the early hours of
14 October 1939, the German submarine U47
slipped through Kirk Sound and torpedoed the
ageing battleship HMS *Royal Oak* with the loss
of 834 lives. Sealing the defences became an
immediate priority, particularly for the First
Lord of the Admiralty, Winston Churchill, and
work began on the Barriers. Aerial cableways
were used to drop wire nets full of rock into
channels which were as much as 18m deep and
whose tides could run at 12 knots. The rock
base was then protected by the concrete cubes
of 5 to 10 tons which give the Barriers their
rugged appearance. Prisoners of war could not
be employed on military projects so the Barriers
became causeways, providing a vital road link
to the South Isles.

Churchill Barriers

48 **Italian Chapel**, Lamb Holm, 1942-4, (see p 70)
Domenico Chiochetti and others
Camp 60 on Lamb Holm was, for much of the
war, home to 550 Italian prisoners of war,
brought to Orkney to supplement the dwindling
civilian labour force on the Barriers. The
Italians were given permission to construct a
chapel in two Nissen huts joined end to end,
and with an extraordinary display of artistry,
craftsmanship and ingenuity, these were
converted into one of Orkney's most beautiful
and unusual buildings. A spiky concrete west
front in red and white was erected, with narrow
Gothic windows, a belfry and a porch featuring
the head of Christ carved on a clay roundel.
Inside, the long barrel-vault of the huts has
been transformed: lined with plasterboard and
painted to resemble vaulted brick and
stonework. The sanctuary is marked off by a
fine wrought-iron screen while altar, altar-rail
and font are cast concrete, the latter featuring
some rather worldly-looking cherubs.

Font, Italian Chapel, Lamb Holm

Sir James Stewart (1694-1746) of Burray was one of the most colourful of Orkney's 18th-century gentry. Forced to flee in 1725 for his part in the murder of Captain Moodie of Melstetter on Broad Street, Kirkwall, he returned to his estate in 1731, having been pardoned. In 1739 while pursuing a deserter who had been removed from Burray by Provost John Riddoch he opened fire with a musket and *lodged its contents in the civic dignitary's seat of honour.* The Earl of Morton who was present had Stewart fined £200 for an attack on *his* person and the proceeds were used to build Kirkwall's Tobooth. Stewart met a somewhat circular fate when in 1746 he was arrested for his part in the '45 by Benjamin Moodie, son of the late Captain, and became the first important prisoner in the Tolbooth for which he had paid. He died in Southwark Gaol later that year.

Chiochetti's painting of the Madonna and Child over the altar (based on that of Nicolo Barabino) dominates, its bright colours lit from the windows at either side. Chiochetti had already demonstrated his artistry in the concrete statue of St George slaying the dragon which marks the position of the camp 'square'.

BURRAY

With three headlands facing north, east and west the low and fertile island of Burray is roughly T-shaped. The broad bay to the east at the Bu is edged by a beautiful sandy beach while that on the west is headed by a narrow gravel spit: a natural barrier which separates Echnaloch from the sea.

49 **Bu**, 18th century
The present house of the Bu rises through three plain well-proportioned and rendered storeys behind the dunes of Bu sands. Remnants of the 17th-century house of James Stewart are scattered through the surrounding walls and outbuildings.

50 **Burray Village** grew up mainly in the 19th century as a herring-fishing community, although its importance dwindled after First World War blockships in Water Sound cut off its direct access to the North Sea. The village's boatbuilding yard has been owned by the same family for five generations.

Sands Motel, 1860
Standing above the pier is a long rectangular two-storey former herring store, packing and curing house in variegated local stone with sandstone dressings.

Storehouse, 1645
Bearing a dated putt stone, this long, low blank-walled grain store has an external stair, and would have stored grain for the Burray estate.

SOUTH RONALDSAY

As the nearest island to the coast of mainland Scotland, South Ronaldsay was the traditional crossing point to Orkney and looked as much to Caithness as to Kirkwall in its trade. It is 12km from north to south; its east coast has a rocky succession of headlands and shallow bays, while on the west, long headlands enclose the beautiful and sheltered expanse of Widewall

Below *Bu.* Bottom *Sands Motel*

Burgher

Burgher

Bay. Most of it is highly productive farmland but moorland around Ward Hill reaches 119m.

51 St Peter's, 1801

Originally dating from 1642, this long and narrow church is beautifully sited on a promontory between two east-facing headlands. It features round-headed windows in its seaward wall and a bellcote while the churchyard and church wall contain a number of 17th- and 18th-century gravestones.

52 St Margaret's Hope

The first recorded inhabitant of *Sanct Margarettis hop* was Thomas Cromartie, mentioned in Rentals of 1589 who must have been involved in trading activities. With the preponderance of trade on the east coast, many ships on passage to and from the north would shelter at the 'Hope' as it is known locally and would require provisions.

In the 19th century, the Hope became a herring station in the boom years of that industry although it never reached the importance of its near neighbour, Burray. St Margaret's Hope was always more important as a centre of communications than a fishing port, owing to its rich agricultural hinterland on South Ronaldsay. It was a port of call for the mail steamer which sailed daily to Scrabster from Stromness via Scapa. With the change of the ferry route, direct to Stromness and the building of the Barriers the Hope's importance dwindled.

The *New Statistical Account* records that *in 1832, the parishioners offered to put a loft in North Church to accommodate 250 people ... but some of the other heritors discouraged the proposals. Baptists have, in consequence, invaded the parish.*

In December 1263 King Hakon Hakonsson of Norway assembled his fleet – the largest of its time in Europe – in the bay of Ronaldsvoe en route to the Battle of Largs. As the ships lay at anchor they witnessed an eclipse of the sun which came to be regarded as an omen of Hakon's death in the battle and, perhaps, of the decline from that point of Norse influence in Orkney and Scotland.

In 1290, Margaret, the seven year-old maid of Norway and heir to the Scottish throne, died in or near Orkney on her journey to Scotland thereby thwarting a plan to marry her to the future Edward II of England. By tradition it was in Ronaldsvoe that she died and the bay – or in Norse, *hop* – became named after her. More prosaically it is suggested that the *hop* was the site of a chapel dedicated, to Malcolm Canmore's Queen, St Margaret. In any event, the anglicised version comes to us today as St Margaret's Hope.

Front Road, St Margaret's Hope

Blaikie Brehner

*Swanson House, Lairdene and
St Margaret's House*

In the early 1900s it was stated
that *The village of St Margaret's
Hope will stand favourable
comparison with places of a similar
size in any part of Scotland. It does
not consist of a collection of fisher
cabins or tumble-down hovels, but of
substantial two-storey houses, some
of them having shops in the lower
areas which would do no discredit to
towns of larger proportions. All
classes seem to prosper well; and, for
the convenience of people in business,
the Union Bank of Scotland has a
branch here. There is a resident
physician in the village, where there
is also an hotel.*

Below *Smithy*. Bottom *Store,
St Margaret's Hope*

Swanson House, Lairdene and **St
Margaret's House**, Front Road, 18th century
This group of close-huddled two-and-a-half-
storey merchants' houses, separated by gaps of
only a few inches, marks one of the starting
points of the settlement. Presenting their gables
to the bay, they stood in line with the shore
with piers projecting into the bay like those at
Stromness. Outbuildings on the piers, the 19th-
century two-storey houses which make up the
Bellevue Hotel and the dressed stone **Bank**,
1873, are all built on reclaimed land making up
Front Road . More 18th-century tall,
crowstepped houses make up the foot of Church
Road while the low house which was the **Post
Office** sits behind a wall built out into the bay.
Nineteenth-century buildings make up **Back
Road** and **Cromarty Square**. The **Cromarty
Hall**, 1878, presents a stone gable to the
square, and it is terminated by the 19th-century
low **Smithy** now restored as a museum.

   The **pier**, road and long sea wall which flank
it were built in the late 19th century to allow
steamers between Mainland Orkney and
Mainland Scotland to berth, rather than uplift
passengers from small boats.

St Margaret's Hope Community School,
1990, Orkney Islands Council: L E Sparrow
A spreading pavilion oversailed by a low-
pitched tiled roof.

Gateway, Smiddybanks, 17th century
A heraldic panel, dated 1633 and 1693 and
topped by a pediment with the figure of a
mermaid, surmounts the courtyard gateway
that is the last remnant of David Sutherland's
mansion, its three-storey **Storehouse** on the
shore below.

Quindry House, 1970, Peter Speakman
A bright L-shaped house with sunken living
room and linking corridor having full-height
windows to make the most of sun and views
across Widewall Bay. On the landward side
purplish brick walls are pierced by narrow
windows and the flat roof, carried on laminated
timber beams, was originally turf-covered. Its
linear organisation may reflect the old Orkney
croft but its materials reflect the aesthetic of
the wartime camps.

Roeberry, 1865
A large hilltop picturesque villa with 'lego-brick'
crowsteps and window surrounds and double-

storey bay window; a recent conservatory helps to reduce its height and strong vertical emphasis – so apparent against the flat Orkney skyline.

53 **Balfour Battery**, Hoxa Head, 1940
A pair of twin 6-pounder gun emplacements with rails for loading trolleys and walls shaped by corrugated iron formwork. Cantilevered roofs were added against air attack in 1941: accompanied by a three-storey observation tower. These looming clifftop structures guarded Hoxa Boom: the main entrance to wartime Scapa. Three small concrete searchlight positions with triple vertical slits to focus the beam stand along the cliff edge. The neat little, cast-iron, gas-powered **lighthouse** was erected in 1901 to guide ships in, rather than keep them out.

Roeberry, S Ronaldsay

Meal Mill, Kirkhouse, late 18th century
The original mill, which was in use until 1972, has an enclosed wheel and is roofed in Orkney slate. A taller kiln roof in Welsh slate was added in the late 19th century.

Balfour Battery, S Ronaldsay

54 **Herston**
An attractive fishing hamlet on the southern shore of Widewall Bay, which consists of widely spaced, mostly 18th-century two-storey houses facing the sea across large gardens.

Tomison's Academy, 1851
The *New Statistical Account* records that *William Tomison, a native of South Parish, went into the service of the Hudson's Bay Company about the year 1770 and acquired a considerable fortune, left for the endowment of a*

Top *Tomison's Academy.* Above
St Mary's

Liddle

free school to the inhabitants of the three united parishes. What they got for his money was a severely symmetrical building of three dressed stone wings, with tall ladder-like windows and high chimneys.

55 **St Mary's**, Burwick, 1789
A blank harled exterior houses an interior remodelled in 1898. The churchyard contains 17th-century gravestones, while the church itself is home to a rounded grey whin stone carved with two footprints, probably used in Pictish inauguration ceremonies. There are various local traditions attached to it, which suggest that St Magnus (amongst others) crossed the Pentland Firth on it, although whether this was the inspiration for the ferry crossing nearby is unclear.

Iron Age House, Liddle, *c.*500 BC
The main feature of this small rounded building is the large flagstone and clay-lined tank in the centre of its floor. Stones were heated on the adjacent hearth and then placed in the tank to heat water for cooking, which explains the most common class of Orkney monuments: 'burnt mounds' made up of heaps of burnt and broken stones.

Tomb of the Eagles, Isbister, *c.*3000 BC
A long communal tomb, with upright flagstone divisions and four side cells, which has a spectacular clifftop setting. Horn-shaped spur walls to either side of the entrance enclosed a seaward-facing ceremonial courtyard. Some of the human skeletons and the totemic remains of sea-eagles, found within, can be seen at the adjacent farmhouse.
Isbister and Liddle are privately owned but open to the public

56 **Pentland Skerries Lighthouses**, *c.*1830, Robert Stevenson
In 1794 two stone towers were erected by the Commissioners for Northern Lights on Muckle Skerry; 24m and 18m in height with fixed lights, they were visited by Scott in 1814 who noted that they were *too low and on the old construction.* In the 1820s they were rebuilt with freestone from Herston: 30.5m apart with the taller one 36m high and gently tapering. In 1895 the fixed lights, sometimes mistaken for the lights of ships, were replaced by a revolving one on the taller tower.

FLOTTA

A fertile valley runs across Flotta (flat island), between higher heather moorland to the east and west. From the north-west corner, a long arm of land reaches eastwards, sheltering the long inlet on Pan Hope which takes its name from salt pans, worked here in the 17th century.

Port War Signalling Station,
Stanger Head, *c.*1939
A long single-storey brick building, its horizontality is emphasised by the concrete roof slab projecting beneath a parapet and contrasting with the five-storey tower rising over the entrance.

57 **Buchanan Battery**, Flotta, 1940
A typical twin 6-pounder coastal defence battery: it has a concrete gun emplacement deep adjacent magazine, three-storey observation tower with overhanging roof slabs, searchlight positions along the shore and a generator house formed by a concrete enclosed Nissen hut.

Buchanan Battery, Flotta

58 **Oil Terminal**, Flotta, 1974-8
W J Cairns & Partners, Moira & Moira
The impact of Occidental's Flotta Terminal on Orkney's economy has been immense. The terminal, which handles 10% of the UK's oil output from seven North Sea fields, carries out initial processing and stores the oil for transfer to visiting tankers; employs about 250 people, 80% of whom are locals; and at its peak has seen a throughput of more than 400,000 barrels a day. It has generated employment and wealth which have helped maintain Orkney's

The Flotta Terminal and some of its neighbours

Flotta Terminal Top *Loading Arms.*
Above *Storage tank*

population and prosperity over the last decade and will continue to do so well into the next century.

However, the impact on the physical environment has been much less dramatic, thanks largely to the early involvement of Orkney Islands Council, who persuaded the oil company to base its operations on the then declining island of Flotta, thereby limiting the extent of environmental upheaval. 'Oxy', in turn, went to some lengths to ensure that the complex was sited and landscaped so as to reduce its prominence in views from all around Scapa Flow. The care taken to protect the environment has now been recognised by a Premier Award from the Association for the Protection of Rural Scotland and a Gold Award from the Business and Industry Panel for the Environment.

On Flotta itself the terminal is an alien presence: the roar of the flare-stack (the terminal's most prominent feature) disturbs the usual tranquillity of the islands and the towers of the gas-processing facility loom at the end of the beautiful inlet of Pan Hope. However, the complex plumbing and stark utilitarianism of the structures give them a singular presence in this bleak corner of the islands. Occidental are committed to reinstatement of the site when it finally closes sometime next century, but it will continue to represent an important stage in Orkney's social and economic history, as did the kelp stores, herring stations and gun batteries which preceded it.

Coastal Defence Battery, Innan Neb, 1940
A twin 6-pounder gun emplacement with attendant observation tower and two smaller 12-pounder emplacements with built-in concrete roofs and mounting rings graduated to give bearings: a searchlight position with triple slit windows also sits on the cliff edge.

HOY & WALLS (see p 71)
Hoy, the high island, is the second largest in the group and consists of the parishes of Hoy in the north and Walls to the south: originally known by its Norse name of *Waas* or *Bays* but inappropriately 'descotticised' by over-zealous mapmakers. South Walls is virtually a separate island linked only by a narrow 'aith' to the rest of Hoy: low lying and green it is much like the rest of Orkney but the ground rises steadily to the north and west to form a more Highland

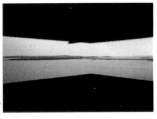

Left *3MW Wind Generator, Burgar Hill.* Above *Churchill Barriers and Scapa Flow from Holm Battery.* Below *Corrigal Farm Museum, Harray.* Bottom *Broch of Gurness, Evie*

Opposite: Top *Italian Chapel.*
Left *Creelboat off Rousay.* Right
Dwarfie Stane, Hoy.
Bottom *Westray from Papa Westray*

This Page: Top left *Balfour Castle:
drawing room.* Left *Hoy cliffs.*
Top *Cottage on Eday.* Above *Stove
and Scar, Sanday: 19th-century
model farms.* Below *Brodgar,
Stenness*

Right *North Ronaldsay Lighthouse.*
Below *Linklet Bay.* Bottom *North
Ronaldsay from the Lighthouse*

landscape reaching 479m at Ward Hill. Along its southern and western edges runs an almost unbroken wall of cliffs which includes the famous 137m stack, the Old Man of Hoy, and rises to more than 300m at St John's Head. The southern part of Walls is reasonably populous and there are other small clusters of settlement at North Hoy and Rackwick, but for the most part the island is heather-covered moorland inhabited only by Arctic Skuas, Great Skuas or 'bonxies', Manx Shearwaters and Peregrine Falcons.

59 **Cantick Head Lighthouse**, 1858, David & Thomas Stevenson
A 22m white-painted brick tower with a stone corbelled walkway, whose light marks the southern approach to Scapa Flow. A long double range of keepers' single-storey houses, stands beside the tower within a stone-walled compound. The flat-roofed octagonal building near the gate housed the foghorn which was used from 1913 to 1987.

Moodie Burial Vault,
Osmundwall Churchyard, 17th century
The small oblong building has a round-headed doorway with an inscribed moulded arch and a tiny pointed window over it. Osmundwall churchyard contains Ian Scott's bronze statue of a lifeboatman in memory of the Longhope Lifeboat: the ill-fated *TGB* which was overturned off South Ronaldsay in 1969 with the loss of all eight of its crew, leaving seven widows and ten orphans in the South Walls community.

60 **Hackness Battery**, S Walls, 1814, Major James Carmichael Smith
The initial response by the Admiralty, to the proposal to build a battery at Longhope, was to ask 'Where is it?' During the Napoleonic Wars, however, it was an important stopping-off point for ships sailing round the north coast to avoid the hazards of the English Channel. Yet, even here, there was danger from American privateers. To protect the anchorage the decision to build a battery was taken. Walter Scott visited the 'fort' as it was being built and noted that it was *A fleche to the sea, with eight guns, 24-pounders, but without any land defences; the guns are mounted en barbette, without embrasures.* In 1866 these were changed for four 68-pounders, anchored to

Below *Cantick Head Lighthouse, S Walls*. Bottom *Osmundwall*

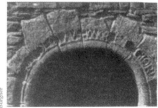

The **Viking Asmundsvagr** is the place where Orkney's Norse rulers were introduced to Christianity. King Olaf Tryggvason, returning home to Norway, came upon Earl Sigurd here. Recently baptised himself, he informed Sigurd that he wanted the Earl and his subjects baptised or *I'll have you killed on the spot, and I swear that I'll ravage every island with fire and steel.* Naturally, Sigurd complied.

Top and above *Hackness Martello Tower*

massive stone blocks, and embrasures were added to the parapet. Between the two pairs of gun emplacements is a thick-walled magazine with a small arms store at either end. Behind it stands slit-windowed barracks.

Martello Towers, Hackness and Crowness, 1815

These gun towers were named after Cape Mortella in Corsica, where, in 1794, a small round tower with a single gun held the Royal Navy at bay for long enough to persuade them of its efficiency to the extent that over 100 were built in Britain; the only other one in Scotland being at Leith. The massive 10m high sandstone tower is oval in plan, being thicker towards the sea, and tapers inwards. The entrance is 4m from the ground and would have been reached by a retractable ladder. A domed chamber housed the gun crews: the officers having their quarters partitioned off. Stairs within the walls lead up to the gun mounting; and down to a magazine, with a water tank to collect water from the roof.
Hackness Tower is open to visitors

61 LONGHOPE

The 'Long Bay' (*hop-bay in Old Norse*), formed between North and South Walls, gave the village its name and its importance as an anchorage, particularly during the Napoleonic Wars. Scott, visiting in 1814, was prompted to write: *Longhope will one day turn out a flourishing place; there will soon be taverns and slop-shops, where sailors rendezvous in such numbers; then will come quays, docks and warehouses; and then a thriving town.* Sadly, the focus of Scapa Flow's shipping later altered; to Stromness, briefly to Lyness and to Flotta. It is a straggling village spread along the southern shore, its focus on the pier at South Ness where the short crossing used to be made to North Walls.

Francis Groome recalls that *in the French war it was no uncommon thing for a fleet of upwards of a hundred large vessels to be lying windbound in this harbour; and a fine sight it was to see them spread their canvas to the breeze and more majestically along the shores of the island.*

Custom House, Longhope, early 19th century
A U-shaped block with wooden-canopied domestic entrances to the side and an official one to the front flanked by pillars bearing a small canopy surmounted by two diminutive lions asserting a cautious authority in this northern outpost.

62 **Melsetter House**, 1898, W R Lethaby
Thomas Middlemore inherited a fortune from a
Birmingham leather business and was able to
retire, with his wife Theodosia, to Orkney.
Having rented Westness on Rousay, they
bought the Melsetter Estate which covered
most of Hoy and commissioned alterations to
the old house of the Moodies to form a
comfortable Edwardian residence. New and old
are kept distinct but the scale and materials –
harling, sandstone dressings, crowsteps and
Caithness slate roofs – sit comfortably in the
Orkney landscape in a way that its Victorian
predecessors were never intended to. Lethaby's
interest in symbolism is evident in the stylised
stone hearts and crescents high on the gables
while his Arts & Crafts background managed to
show through; particularly in the small-paned
mullioned windows and the triple dormer to the
north-east.

The entrance opens from a sunny courtyard
into a spacious hall with a large arched
fireplace with corbelled candlestick supports.
The bright, L-shaped drawing room with
simple, square white-painted panelling lies to
the north-east. French windows and an elegant
outside stair lead to the garden, and a high
window lets in the late afternoon sun. Dining
room and library also open off the hall and the
stairs lead to bedrooms above and service areas
below. Other rooms open off corridors running
along the courtyard on ground and first floors,
and enjoy the views across the garden to the
sea. The house was a relaxed, open and
democratic one; with the servants' quarters
overlooking the garden. Furnishings were

May Morris described Melsetter as
*a sort of fairy palace on the edge of
the northern sea, a wonderful place ...
remotely and romantically situated,
with its tapestries and its silken
hangings and its carpets; for all its
fineness and dignity it was a place
full of homeliness and the spirit of
welcome, a very lovable place. And
surely that is the test of an architect's
genius; he built for home life as well
as for dignity.*

Top *Courtyard*. Above *Drawing
Room*. Below *Melsetter policies*

N E Elevation, Melsetter

Chapel of SS Margaret and Colm

William Richard Lethaby (1857-1931) was one of the leading figures in the Arts & Crafts Movement, although he actually built very little, being more concerned latterly with design education. Having won the Soane Medallion he became an employee of, and then principal assistant to, Norman Shaw, before establishing his own practice in 1889. His house at Avon Tyrrell, Hampshire (1891) is in the English domestic revival style pioneered by William Morris and Philip Webb while his All Saints Church (1900-2) at Brockhampton in Herefordshire has been described as *probably the most original church of its date in the world*. In 1894 he became the founding Principal of the Central School of Arts and Crafts in London; the first to include craft workshops as advocated by Morris; and later Professor of Design at the Royal College of Art. He did much to establish formal architectural education and his views were influential, most notably in Germany and the United States. An advocate of conservation rather than restoration he was a leading member of Morris's Society for the Protection of Ancient Buildings.

largely by Morris & Co, including Morris fabrics and carpets and designs by George Jack, W A S Benson, Ernest Gimson, Ford Maddox Brown, Philip Webb and Lethaby himself; and a few pieces remain in the house.

Chapel of St Margaret & St Colm, Melsetter, 1900, W R Lethaby
The gable of this little chapel is the south-east wall of the entrance courtyard and it is reached from there via a steep flight of steps. In contrast with the refined elegance of the house, it has bare rubble walls and a steep Gothic-arched vault in board-marked concrete, covered in Caithness slate. A prototype for his famous church at Brockhampton. Lethaby's love of symbolism is demonstrated in the stylised sun, moon and cross on the keystone of the low arched door and in the wave pattern round the geometric and monolithic stone font. Stained glass is by Christopher Whall, Burne-Jones and Ford Maddox Brown.

Estate Buildings, 1898, W R Lethaby
A one-sided street leading up from the house,
the old farm buildings have been treated as
part of an integrated complex with it. All are
rendered and roofed traditionally, while the
estate office has a massive sandstone porch in
the shape of an upturned boat, sheltering
outdoor seats.

Garrison Theatre, N Walls

Garrison Theatre, *c.*1942
The art deco black-rendered brickwork and
white-banded windows of this frontage
disguised the huge Nissen hut which stood
behind it. With more than 20,000 servicemen
and women stationed on the island in 1943 and
the bleakness and remoteness of the posting,
the provision of entertainment was essential. It
is now a guest house.

North Walls School & Community Centre,
1985, Orkney Islands Council Architects:
M M Gilbertson and L E Sparrow
On the site of a former farm, the school has to
some extent maintained the appearance of a
domestic and agricultural complex. Pitched,
tiled roofs, render and domestic windows help
to achieve this although the resulting building
lacks the kind of institutional presence which it
might deserve.

Below *Piers, Lyness.*
Bottom *Pump House*

63 **LYNESS**
In two World Wars Lyness formed the hub of
the Royal Navy's base in Scapa Flow: its
sheltered bay providing a harbour for the
important tasks of replenishing and refuelling
ships and maintaining the steel anti-submarine
nets which were hung across the entrances to
the Flow. Tangible reminders of all this activity
lie all around in the abandoned concrete and
brick buildings: heightening the bleakness of
Hoy's landscape.

Pumping Station, 1917
First World War truss-roofed sheds house the
steam pumps which used to drive fuel oil up
from the piers into storage tanks. Originally
coal-powered, the boilers were converted to oil-
firing in 1936. They are housed in a large bright
shed and their brick plinths make ideal display
space for the Interpretation Centre established
here since 1985. The concrete area in front of
the pump house was used to lay out the anti-
submarine nets hauled ashore over the ramp
near the ferry terminal. *Open to the public:
leaflet available*

Oil Tank, Lyness, 1917
The survivor of four 12,000-ton oil tanks, the vast echoing chamber of the empty tank is spanned by spidery trusses in a star arrangement and awaits a new use. In 1936 twelve more 15,000-ton tanks, now demolished, were added and work began to hollow out the Hill of Wee Fea, the hill behind the harbour, to provide a further 100,000 tons of oil storage. The first tank was completed only in 1942 and the sixth and final one in August 1943. The only visible signs of this abandoned facility are two tunnel mouths and the deep-water quay which was formed from the spoil and named Golden Wharf because of the cost of its construction.

Sheds, Lyness, c.1918
The huge area covered by these red painted sheds, their roofs carried on successive rows of curved Belfast trusses, was the inter-war home of Cox & Danks and Metal Industries, the salvage firms which raised the scuttled German fleet. However, in February 1940 they served as the Lyness Naafi and the largest cinema in Europe, graced by stars such as Vera Lynn, George Formby and Flannigan and Allan.

Communications Centre, Wee Fea, 1943
A blocky concrete building on the hillside with portholes for windows and a signalling bridge, this was the control centre for the anchorage.

Rysa Lodge, 1904, W R Lethaby
A residence for the Middlemores' shooting guests, this long, low two-storey house is based around an older cottage, which became the caretaker's wing to the rear. The tiny windows on the north elevation open into a corridor linking the south-facing rooms. Traditional in style, details such as its paired windows indicate its Arts & Crafts pedigree.

64 **Burra House**, N Hoy, 1798
A substantial former manse of two storeys and an attic which shelters in a walled garden by the shore. Walter Scott took tea here when returning from his visit to the Dwarfie Stane. A range of outbuildings terminates in a particularly finely built stone kiln.

Bu of Hoy, c.1615
An important site since Viking times, the two-storey house with its three crowstepped dormers was originally built for the Halcros.

Below *Rysa Lodge*.
Bottom *Burra House, Hoy*

Much altered, it still has a puttstone bearing the initials H.H.

Dwarfie Stane, 3000-2000 BC (see p 70)
Appearing from the road as just a tiny chip from the 'hamars' behind it, this rock-cut tomb consists of a short passage and two kerbed side chambers carved from the heart of a sandstone boulder measuring roughly 10m x 5m x 2.4m. Orkney's most unusual tomb and the one which has most exercised the minds and pens of its visitors. *Open to the public*

The Dwarfie Stane was described by Jo Ben in the 16th century as *a stone that merits wonder ... fashioned by a giant and his wife*, although the 'giant' must have been particularly diminutive if this was to have been his bed. Scott, rather more consciously, fitted fiction to it by making it the place in which Norna of the Fitful Head, the witch of *The Pirate*, meets the *misshapen form of the necromantic owner ... Trolld, a dwarf famous in the Northern Sagas* and undergoes her translation to supernatural powers.

65 **Rackwick**
This beautiful solitary valley opens directly on to the Atlantic, which has thrown up massive rounded boulders on to the curving beach from which cliffs rise to 175m to the east. Once it held a scattered crofting community who eked out a living here. Its population, which had dwindled to one, is now back in double figures, including Manchester-born composer, Sir Peter Maxwell Davies. Many of the abandoned crofts have also become holiday homes, whether by careful conservation in traditional materials or by construction in corrugated iron or asbestos.

Burnmouth Cottage, 19th century *(above)*
Renovated by the Hoy Trust as a bothy for visitors, this long low cottage displays two traditional roofing forms: flagstones on the outbuilding and a thatch covering on the house held down by heather ropes or 'simmans' weighted with stones. The yard is surrounded by a rough wall of beach stones.

Top *Dwarfie Stane*. Above *Rackwick*

66 **GRAEMSAY**
Hoy High and **Hoy Low Lighthouses**, 1851, Alan Stevenson
This pair of white-painted stone towers was built to guide ships into Hoy Sound from the west. **Hoy High**, the Rolls-Royce of Orkney's

Hoy Low

A broad and beautiful sound or strait, wrote Scott, *divided this lonely and mountainous island [Hoy] from Pomona [Mainland], and in the centre of that sound lies, like a tablet composed of emerald, the beautiful and verdant island of Graemsay.*

lighthouses, is an elegant 33m tower on the east coast of the island with its gallery carried on Gothic-arched corbels. Inside it features angel statuettes and lamp room ventilators decorated with the classical faces of wind gods; while the flat-roofed single-storey houses have massive projecting door surrounds and tall tapering chimneys. In the true spirit of late Georgian eclecticism, these are said to have been based upon Egyptian temples. **Hoy Low's** lamp room and gallery barely rise above its shortened tower's pedimented doorway; the adjacent Second World War battery observation tower almost dwarfing it.

NORTH ISLES
More scattered than the South Isles and separated by often stormy channels, the North

Netherhouse, Westray

Isles are notable mainly for their agriculture which through 19th-century estate improvement gave them some of the best farms in Orkney. Economic pressures and isolation have led to depopulation and slow decline, and particularly in the smaller islands, the lilting Orcadian accent has often been replaced by the voice of southern Britons, seeking an escape to island remoteness and a different way of life – all too often to find the pressures just as great, if different in nature.

SHAPINSAY
The south-west corner of Shapinsay lies just over 1km across the String from Carness, outside Kirkwall, and from there it is only 14km to its north-east extremity. Although relatively flat, the island rises gently to low cliffs on the east coast. The Shapinsay landscape, however, owes much to the straight

roads and relentless field grid imposed by its mid 19th-century laird, David Balfour.

67 **Balfour Castle**, begun 1847, David Bryce
Thomas Balfour bought the estate of Sound in 1782 and had the house of Cliffdale built on it. In 1846 it passed to his grandson, David Balfour WS, along with the title Balfour of Trenaby and a considerable family fortune made by his great-uncle in India. Balfour immediately engaged Bryce, who had lately taken charge of William Burn's Scottish practice, thereby giving the Edinburgh architect his first major opportunity to design a country house in his own right. The arrangement adheres to a formula widely used and developed by Bryce. The old house is sandwiched between a service wing to the north and a three-storey wing of public rooms to the south, with dining room, drawing room and library arranged off a picture gallery. The drawing room on the corner makes the most of the sun and views to the south and links to the garden via a conservatory to the west. A classical interior contrasts with a Baronial exterior, with crowstepped gables, square and conically roofed towers and turrets.

Top *Balfour Castle (see p 71)*. Above *Gatehouse*

Gateway, Sound, 1647
The only remnant of Sound, home of the Buchanans, burnt to the ground in 1746 to punish Patrick Fea, captor of *Pirate Gow*, for his part in the Jacobite Rising. Its round arch is flanked by pairs of Corinthian columns and topped by an armorial panel bearing the arms and initials of Arthur Buchanan and his wife. It now serves as a sheltered seat in the garden of Balfour.

Dishan Tower

Dishan Tower, 17th century
A tall round stone tower guarding the entrance to Elwick Bay; it was designed as a doocot but was converted in the 19th century to form a salt-water shower.

Gatehouse, 1851, David Bryce
A castellated porter's lodge forming part of the mock defences constructed around the harbour. It now serves as the island's bar.

Balfour Village
Sheltered by the island of Heliar Holm, Elwick Bay provides a safe natural anchorage. It was here that King Haakon Haakonson's great fleet lay on St Olaf's Day 1263, *en route* to the Battle

Balfour Village

of Largs. In the late 18th century the village of Shoreside was built for workers on the Cliffdale Estate but by the mid 19th century, David Balfour had renamed it and had the southern part demolished to improve the approach to his new house. With gardens on the opposite side of the road running down to the sea, it retains a pleasantly unified appearance as the only planned village in Orkney. The **Smithy**, *c.*1850, now housing a museum and restaurant has a stone forestair, the doorway marked by a crowstepped gable and the main elevation further enlivened by dormered windows. This was originally the north end of the village and marked the approach road to Sound. The village is terminated by a **Gateway**, *c.*1850, by David Bryce: a pair of two-storey houses whose gables flank the free-standing ashlar pillars which mark the northern approach to Balfour Estate.

Gasometer, 19th century
Another apparent fortification; a round rubble-built tower with red-brick parapet, built to supply gas to both house and village. Stones from Noltland Castle (dated 1725) have been built into it.

Elwick Bank

Mill, 19th century
An imposing structure, three storeys high with a single dormered window over its freestone-arched doorway. The large overshot wheel is still intact and twin kiln vents pierce the roof.

Elwick Bank, 1812
Built by David Balfour's father for two aunts. A fine white-rendered Georgian house with niched outhouses, standing aloof from the village above the opposite shore of the bay.

Lady Kirk, 1656
A fragment of an earlier (1630) church, erected by Major George Buchanan of Sound whose initials and the date appear on carved stones. It later became the Balfours' burial chapel.

ROUSAY (see p 70)
Rousay lies off the north of the West Mainland and is the high island of the North Isles, its flagstone layers weathered to a series of hills of stepped profile, which reach 250m at Blotchnie Fiold. Much of it is unproductive moorland: the more so because it was the only island to suffer Highland-style evictions in the 19th century. Settlement took place in lower-lying coastal ground between the high shoulders of the island and began at an early date with a group of prehistoric tombs, which have earned Rousay the epithet 'Egypt of the North'.

68 **Trumland House**, 1870-3, David Bryce
A gaunt Jacobean-style mansion, likened to *a polished black and white dice* by Edwin Muir. It was built for the diminutive Lt-General Frederick William Traill Burroughs, who retired to his Westness Estate having achieved distinction in the army in India. Introduced to Bryce in 1870 by David Balfour, he was promised *a very compact, complete and nice-looking house ... for £3000 or less*. As at Balfour's Shapinsay residence, the principal rooms are on the first floor and the lofty corner drawing room with its huge windows commands glorious views over the surrounding islands. The house is set in 50 acres of plantations and gardens.

Taversoe Tuick, *c.*3500 BC
A communal tomb, comprising two stone-wal 82 ed chambers built one on top of the other separated by a floor of thick stone slabs and entered by separate passages leading from uphill and downhill sides of the mound. The original roof has been replaced by a shallow concrete dome with central oculus. *Open to the public*

Blackhammer Cairn, *c.*3500 BC
A tomb of the stalled variety peculiar to Orkney, with pairs of upright flagstones dividing a long dry-stone passage. The modern concrete roof is almost Corbusian in form, contrasting strongly with the ancient structure it protects. **Knowe of Yarso**, *c.*3500 BC, is

Building and furnishing
Trumland cost Burroughs £10,374, partly responsible for debts which inspired him to become the most notorious of the islands' landlords. The ensuing dispute with crofting tenants reached the national press, caused a gunboat to be sent to Rousay and an Act of Parliament to be passed to prevent his circumvention of the Crofting Act. Like his house, Burroughs did not fit comfortably into the Orkney landscape.

Below *Trumland House*. Bottom *Blackhammer Cairn*

Hullion

similar in form but shorter and taller, occupying a spectacular setting on top of one of the rocky outcrops which give Rousay's slopes their characteristic stepped outline. *Open to the public*

Hullion, 17th-19th century
A small group of stone farm buildings, houses, cottages and watermill grouped picturesquely along the road beside a small burn. The oldest part is now almost obscured by ivy and is used as a coalshed but has been a substantial two-storey house in its day with an external stone stair.

Westness House, 1792
Originally the principal house on Rousay: two narrow floors and a partial attic storey marked on the seaward elevation by a circular window. Extensive walled gardens with a plantation owe their present form to Burroughs who purchased the house in 1863, re-roofing and extending it in 1872. A small chapel constructed within the former boiler house for the greenhouses dates from the 1920s. Burroughs occupied the house until moving to Trumland whose Baronial splendour better suited his pretensions than the homely elegance of Westness. In the 1890s it was let to the Middlemores, later of Melsetter, who redecorated with Arts & Crafts wallpapers and fireplace tiles. **Viera Lodge**, 18th century, was the factor's residence.

St Mary's Church, Swandro, 12th century
A roofless chapel tilting alarmingly against buttresses added in the late 19th century, and incorporating the remains of two aumbries.

Below *Westness*. Bottom *Revolving summerhouse*

Wirk, 12th century
The remains of a square tower constructed of large rectangular stone blocks mark the western end of what was probably a Norse hall. A stair curves under it at the east side, possibly to a former well, while the wall contains a gardrobe flue.

Midhowe Tomb, c.3500 BC
A massive communal stalled tomb with eleven pairs of upright flagstones, housed in a sturdily built, stone-walled 1930s hangar whose arched trusses carry a walkway giving an overhead view. The effect is rather like that of a whale's skeleton in a museum and the smaller tombs are worth visiting for their greater accessibility. *Open to the public*

69 **Midhowe Broch**, *c.*200BC-AD200
A well-preserved specimen of an Iron Age
fortified house sited on a promontory and
protected by a ditch and rampart to the
landward side. The circular wall survives to a
height of 4.3m and contains galleries at ground
floor. It originally would have had a timber
sleeping floor at first-floor level, supported on a
stone ledge 3m up the inside of the wall. The
interior was divided into two rooms by upright
flagstones in a later occupation. Houses outside
the tower provided accommodation in times of
safety with the broch serving as a refuge. *Open
to the public*

Tafts, Quendale, 15th century
The ruined remains of one of the oldest two-
storey houses in Orkney which served as the
centre of the crofting township of Quendale. The
sixteen households of this exposed valley were
cleared by George William Traill in 1845.

Mill, 19th century
Now a dwelling house but originally a three-
storey rubble-walled watermill which still
features a projecting external timber sack hoist,
unique in Orkney watermills. The kiln features
four date stones.

EGILSAY
Barely 5km in length, 'Egil's Island', low and
green but with an uneven topography, lies east
of Rousay and was the site of the martyrdom of
St Magnus in *c.*1117.

70 **St Magnus Church**, *c.*1136
Erected possibly to mark the martyrdom site
after the recognition of Magnus's sanctity, it
has a rectangular nave and smaller chancel,
the latter having a barrel vault with an attic
chamber above, reached from a nave gallery
and used probably as a store for the church's
valuables. The massive stonework and narrow,
deeply splayed windows give an impression of
fortification, heightened by the 15m-tall
cylindrical tower at the west end. The tower
was lowered in the early 19th century, as it *was
ruinous and likely to come down*, but it is
recorded as having had a beehive-shaped roof.
Open to the public

WYRE
The island takes is name from its shape, a
'spearhead' or Norse 'vigr'. Low-lying and fertile

Midhowe Broch

**According to the Sagas, cousins
Hakon Paulsson and Magnus
Erlandson** were joint Earls of
Orkney but their relationship
became soured by Hakon's jealousy
of his associates. The Earls agreed to
meet on Egilsay just after Easter
1117, with equal numbers of men
and ships to discuss their differences.
However, Hakon arrived with eight
vessels rather than two and although
Magnus offered to be exiled or
imprisoned, Hakon had him
executed.
Hakon went on to be a respected
ruler who led a crusade to the Holy
Land. Magnus's remains were
interred at Christ Church in Birsay
where a series of miraculous events
and cures began to be reported.
Magnus was made a saint; his relics
transferred to the church in Kirkwall
and later placed in the Cathedral
dedicated to him by his nephew,
where they remain to this day.

St Magnus Church

Cubbie Roo's Castle, Wyre

it is 3km long, and lies to the south-east of Rousay, pointing westwards.

71 'Cubbie Roo's Castle', 12th century

At that time, says the Saga, *there was a very able man named Kolbein Hruga [heap] farming on Wyre. He had a fine stone fort there, a really solid stronghold.* Set on a 25m hill surrounded by a low-lying marsh land, the basement of this structure still survives, rising to a height of about 2m. Later outbuildings of less robust construction surround it and the whole is partly encircled by a ditch cut into the rock. The neighbouring area has probably been farmed since Norse times and provided the childhood home of one of Britain's greatest 20th-century poets **Edwin Muir**. *Open to the public*

St Mary's Chapel, 12th century

Roofless but well preserved, and featuring a rectangular nave and narrower chancel, St Mary's was constructed probably by either Kolbein Heap or his son Bjarni, the third Bishop of St Magnus Cathedral. The rubble walls are pierced by low doorways with semicircular flagstone arches. During excavations the remains of a large man were found: possibly those of Kolbein Heap. *Open to the public*

EYNHALLOW

The 'Holy Isle' lies half-way between Evie and Rousay, cut off by fierce tide races or 'roosts'. Eynhallow was said to have supernatural qualities, in particular the ability to disappear and reappear. Nowadays this behaviour may only be attributed, prosaically, to Atlantic fog.

72 Church, 12th century

When fever broke out in 1851 and the island's inhabitants evacuated, the subsequent dismantling of a two-storey dwelling-house revealed a small Romanesque church, probably at the centre of a monastic settlement. A rectangular nave and chancel are separated by a variety of arched doorways: straight sided, semicircular and Gothic.

GAIRSAY

Gairsay consists of a single 102m hill rising off the shore of Rendall. It was the home of the Viking Svein Asleifarson who kidnapped Earl Paul Hakonarson soon after the arrival in Orkney of Rognvald Kali Kolsson. After an

Edwin Muir, (1887-1959) poet, critic, translator and novelist, was born in Deerness on the Mainland, moving later to the **Bu** on Wyre and then to a farm near Kirkwall. His work, with its heraldic imagery, constantly refers to a lost Eden: the islands he left at fourteen for industrial Glasgow. With his wife, Willa, he travelled widely in Europe and they subsequently translated 43 volumes, notably Kafka's *The Castle, The Trial* and *America* and Brod's *The Sleepwalkers.* After the Second World War, he was appointed director of the British Institute first in Prague, then in Rome, before becoming warden of Newbattle Abbey College near Edinburgh.

This was how Svein used to live: winter he would spend at home on Gairsay, where he entertained some 80 men at his own expense. His drinking hall was so big, there was nothing in Orkney to compare with it. In the spring he had more than enough to occupy him, with a great deal of seed to sow which he saw to carefully himself. Then he would go off plundering in the Hebrides and Ireland, then back home just after midsummer where he stayed until the cornfields had been reaped and the grain was safely in. After that he would go off raiding again.
Orkneyinga Saga

eventful life Svein was killed on a Viking raid shortly after having taken control of the City of Dublin.

73 **Langskaill**, 1676

The remains of one of Orkney's finest small mansion houses mark the site of Svein's hall. A wing to the north of the courtyard has gone and the two-storey western one is ruined but the single-storey east wing was restored in c.1900 and is still inhabited. The seaward side gateway is headed by a pedimented armorial panel with the initials of William Craigie and his wife Margaret Honeyman, for whom the house was built.

STRONSAY

Stronsay (*Strom*, Old Norse: tide race) is virtually two islands. A ridge running south from Huip and encircling Meikle Water forms the main island. Rothiesholm (pronounced Rousam) is joined to it by a narrow neck of sand dunes. To the north, the island of Papa Stronsay shelters the long stretch of Papa Sound, which was Orkney's great fishing harbour of the 19th century. The three long bays, which give the island its distinctive shape, made it pre-eminent in the 18th-century kelp industry.

74 **Whitehall**

The village of Whitehall was founded by Malcolm Laing of Papdale early in the 19th century with the help of a London fisheries company. Stronsay had been exporting live lobsters to London since the late 18th century and cod fishing for export began in 1828, but it was the herring fishing that was to make Whitehall the main Orkney fishing port.

Whitehall consists of three parts. Furthest east is the **Station**; its few houses, mostly single-storey cottages, are largely ruinous.

Lower Whitehall is the site of Malcolm Laing's original fishing station. Its houses, a mixture of traditional one- and two-storey buildings in somewhat better states of repair, are spaced relatively widely along the shore facing northwards across the sea.

The **pierhead** of the modern village marks the approximate position of the 16th-century house of North Strynzie, built for Patrick Fea, whose son James, 1700-30, introduced kelp burning and the house renamed Whitehall. It is from this that the village now takes its name.

RCAHMS

Langskaill

In the 1840s there were up to 400 fishing boats with 25-30 supporting vessels in Stronsay from late July through August as the annual migration of Herring passed Orkney. On Sundays it was said to be possible to walk across to Papa Stronsay on the decks of the boats. Following the fleet came coopers, curers and several hundred women to gut and salt the fish. By the early 1900s, although the industry was declining, Whitehall could boast a cinema and ice cream parlour and a chip shop.

James Fea of Whitehall carried out the first kelp burning in c.1720. Seaweed burned in shallow depressions still dotted around the shores of the islands, yielded ashes rich in soda, potash (used in glass and soap making in the north of England) and iodine. Orkney became the main centre for kelp production in Britain and the industry provided huge profits for the 18th-century lairds, encouraging them to indulge in architectural and agricultural improvement.

Pierhead, Whitehall

Burgher

Fishmarket, Whitehall

Fishmarket, Pierhead, early 20th century
A long slate-roofed building with a rear wall
rising straight out of the harbour.

Stronsay Hotel, Pierhead, 1931; altered 1937
The original hotel, said to have had the longest
bar in the North of Scotland, burned down in
1937. This part of the white rendered house was
pressed into service as a replacement. Behind
the hotel are the remains of four single-storey
corrugated-iron huts built to accommodate
visiting fishermen.
　　The main part of the village, to the west of
the pier, was developed between 1900 and 1910.
Substantial two-storey houses, most with
porches and dormers, face seawards.

Below *Stronsay Hotel,Whitehall.*
Bottom *Boat House, Whitehall*

The **West Pier** was built in the 1930s. Beside it
is a stone-built, seawater-flushed public toilet,
built out on to the shore and reached by a
narrow gangway, and a small **house** roofed
with an upturned boat (complete with stove and
chimney), presaging the 'boat houses' in
Finstown.

Papa Stronsay, the small island lying due
north of the village, still has some of the long
corrugated-iron sheds which provided
dormitories for the fisher girls and the
circular stumps of the chimneys of 19th-century
kelp kilns.

Huip, 18th century
The most prominent house on the approach to
the sheltered anchorage at Papa Sound.
Rendered and roofed in local stone it survived
the destruction of kelp-processing machinery in

the 1742 Kelp Riots. Its occupier in 1814, David Drever, instigated the first herring fisheries on Stronsay.

Water Pumping Station, 1972, Orkney Islands Council

Simple geometry and bright blue paintwork of this installation gives it more architectural presence than most of the islands' recent engineering projects.

75 Moncur Memorial Church, 1955 Leslie Grahame Thomson (MacDougall)

When Alexander Moncur died in 1944 he left £20,000 to build a new church on Stronsay, in memory of his grandfather James Mudie, UP minister from 1822 to 1860. What resulted was the present narrow lofty building, curiously old-fashioned for its date and decidedly un-Presbyterian in form. The Communion Table is set in a sanctuary lit by a stained-glass East Window by Marjorie Kemp of Edinburgh, depicting the Good Shepherd. The sanctuary is floored in grey Sandwick flagstone and flanked by pulpit and prayer desk on red sandstone plinths. Sandstone is also used to support the massive timber roof trusses and trim the tall, narrow windows. The emphasis is on simplicity: natural local materials (both sandstone and flagstone walling are from Rothiesholm), round arches and plain light fittings. The original scheme included a manse and hall arranged round a courtyard with a tall circular tower modelled on St Magnus Church, Egilsay. Unfortunately these were never carried out.

Stronsay Mill, 19th century

In use until recently, the overshot wheel and machinery of this three-storey mill are still in place. A single timber vent protruding through the slate roof marks the position of drying kiln.

76 Mount Pleasant, c.1915

The childhood home of Douglas Sutherland, whose *Against the Wind* describes his life here. Its red sandstone was quarried on Rothiesholm but dressed by masons brought from 'South'. The Sutherland crest with its motto *Sans Peur* is over the door.

Rothiesholm School, 19th century

A neat and tiny one-room school, in local stone and slate; it held seven pupils at the time of its closure after the Second World War.

The well at Kildinguie is situated further along Mill Bay from the pumping station. Water from this source, taken in combination with seaweed from the geo of Odin, was once reputed to have had healing powers, and attracted visitors from as far as Norway and Denmark. The 19th-century suggestion that a spa be developed was, however, never adopted.

Moncur Memorial Church

Below *Mount Pleasant, Stronsay.* Bottom *Rothiesholm School*

77 Auskerry Lighthouse, 1865-7,
Thomas Stevenson
The 34m white-painted brick tower was first lit
on 1 March 1867 to guide ships into the
sheltered anchorages off Stronsay.

SANDAY

At 21km from Spur Ness in the south to the
Tafts Ness in the north, Sanday is the largest of
the North Isles. In the west it rises to 65 km at
the Wart . To the north and east the island is
composed mainly of sand, which gives the
island its name, and barely reaches 15m above
sea level. The old *Statistical Account* attributed
this contrast to the earth's eastward rotation.

Below Warsetter Doocot. *Middle*
Stove. *Bottom* Ortie

78 Kettletoft
Although never as important as Whitehall,
Kettletoft was also a fishing harbour. The
Store at the pierhead is a substantial stone-
built affair on two floors with arched doorway.
Unlike their Whitehall counterparts, the 19th-
century houses turn their backs on the sea: high
stone sea walls dropping to the shore. Closely
huddled two-storey houses at the pierhead tail
off along the road to smaller cottages inland.

Doocot, Warsetter, 17th century
Perched on Sanday's highest hill in the shadow
of the telephone mast, a flagstone-roofed
doocot slopes up from three sides to a north-
facing gable. The 1613 datestone may be from
another building, perhaps the nearby Sinclair
house.

79 Stove, 1860s (see p 71)
A large steading, and one of the first to
introduce mechanisation in the form of a
Clayton & Shuttleworth steam-driven threshing
machine. As a result, its most prominent
feature is the stump of a red brick chimney on
the boiler-house. The adjacent farm buildings
are now sadly in ruins.

80 Ortie, 19th century
A now largely abandoned crofting township
arranged in a remarkably long straight 'kloss'
running down to the sea *built when the land
was squared;* at one time it housed a population
of more than sixty.

81 Scar, Westove, early 19th century (see p 71)
A sprawling two-storey house with dormered
attic and extensive steading. Flagstone roofs
covered in yellow lichen surround a wide

90

Scar House

courtyard. The adjoining range ends in a steam-powered meal mill with its prominent boiler-house and chimney still intact. The lean-to **doocot** and 3m-high enclosed garden walls all bear testimony to the prominence of the Westove Estate. The squat tapering circular stone tower of a **windmill** stands close by. Water power was not widely available in Sanday, leading a 19th-century writer to observe that *formerly there were a number of windmills in the island, which at a distance from shore looked as if they rose out of the sea, owing to the flatness of the land.*

Patrick Neill in 1805 *visited the house of Scar, the seat of Mr Traill of Westove who resides on his property and is engaged in inclosing, draining and other improvements. Here we were happy to find a most extensive library, which must be a source of great pleasure to an enlightened mind during the dreary months of winter in this lonely insular situation.*

82 **Start Point Lighthouse**, 1870
After the building of Orkney's first lighthouse on North Ronaldsay, ships which had previously kept well to the east of the islands made for the new light, bringing them dangerously close to low-lying Sanday. As a result, an unlit beacon topped with a ball of masonry was erected in 1802, on the most easterly point of Sanday. A revolving light, of the type that impressed Robert Stevenson on his tour of English lighthouses, was fitted in 1806; the first in Scotland. The original squarish two-storey block of flat-roofed keepers' houses still stands but Stevenson's telescope-like ashlar tower, depicted by Daniell in 1821, was replaced by a 21m brick structure in 1870, subsequently painted with striking vertical black and white bands.

Below *Lighthouse on the Start, Isle of Sanday.* Bottom *Lodge, Geramount*

Tresness, 19th century
A substantial steading that includes a covered horse-gang whose octagonal pyramidal roof is a departure from the conical versions favoured elsewhere in the islands.

Geramount, 1835
The hipped roof has gone, but it has clearly been an elegant and well-proportioned late-Georgian house, with an advanced centre bay.

Geramount, Sanday

Burgher

The Revd Alexander Goodfellow, wrote *There is no better house in all the island than Geramount, well built, well seen, and well known. For situation there is nothing to match it, a city set upon a hill, an object that attracts the eye.* It was built for John Traill Urquhart, who had married into the wealthy Traill family. Urquhart did not, however, live to appreciate it. In 1835 a fight broke out in Kirkwall over a disputed election result, in the course of which he received a blow to the kidneys which exacerbated an existing illness and killed him.

Below *Carrick House.*
Bottom *Lodge, Carrick, Eday*

It was originally set in 100 acres laid out as a park, guarded by an octagonal-ended **cottage**, a particularly neat essay in Orkney stone with flagstones projecting over windows and door.

EDAY (see p 71)
Taking its name from the broad sandy isthmus 'aith' which divides the island, Eday is just over 17km long from north to south and lies at the centre of the North Isles. The flagstone bedrock is overlaid with sandstone. As a result, much of the island is agriculturally unproductive hill land, rising to 101m at Ward Hill. Although this geology is not appropriate to farming, it has given the island two of its major exports in the past. Peat was shipped to the other islands (especially Sanday and North Ronaldsay which have no moss of their own) and from 1926 to 1945 the Eday Peat Company exported to Scottish distillers as far away as Leith, having built railway tracks to carry their product down to Carrick Bay. Eday sandstone was used in the building of St Magnus Cathedral, and Eday was the source of much of the decorative freestone in the islands. Few modern buildings have intruded, giving one of the best-preserved pictures of Orkney crofts as they were after the agricultural improvements of the 19th century.

83 **Carrick House**, 1633 and later
Stands by the shore of the anchorage of Calf Sound, oriented to the sea. The harled and crowstepped gable of the original house of John Stewart, Lord Kinclaven, rises through two storeys and an attic almost directly from the foreshore, and the original arched courtyard gateway faces northward to the Red and Grey Heads across the sheltered curve of the narrow strait. Its date is carved on the keystone of the arch while the kitchen, sited across the courtyard, is probably in what remains of an even older house. On the death of Kinclaven, younger brother of Earl Patrick Stewart, the house passed to the Buchanans and the armorial panel over the gate bears the initials of Arthur Buchanan and his wife, matching that of their house at **Sound** in Shapinsay. Later it was the home of James Fea of Clestrain, captor of the pirate John Gow. In 1853 the estate was bought by Robert James Hebden. Although he apparently contemplated the 'baronialisation' of his new home, he eventually settled for a more low-key approach, building virtually a second house next to it in matching crowstepped style and linking them

at ground-floor level by a low passage. As a result, Carrick constitutes a particularly good example of a 17th-century laird's house, although what appear to be original fireplaces in the north gable are in fact 1930s reinstatements.

Cottages, Carrick, *c.*1855
The Hebdens' summer expeditions to their northern retreat were accompanied by a retinue which included a butler and coachman, who were accommodated in two well-proportioned cottages with tall central chimney stacks and hipped roofs in Eday sandstone.

Stone of Setter *(below)*
The most spectacular single standing stone in Orkney, this heavily weathered and lichen-covered monolith has taken on the appearance of a huge hand reaching out of the ground. *Open to the public*

John Gow, the son of a Caithness immigrant to Orkney was, late in 1724, the second mate of a vessel called the *George* off the Barbary Coast. When the captain was killed in a mutiny, Gow took command and, having renamed the ship the *Revenge*, embarked on a career of piracy. After an unpromising start Gow sailed homeward and, following an abortive attack on the Hall of Clestrain, found his ship aground on the Calf of Eday. James Fea managed to take a first landing party, and then Gow himself, prisoner. After only a few months Gow's exploits led him to the execution dock but he was to achieve immortality of sorts when Scott used his story as the basis of *The Pirate*: a novel of only passing literary interest but containing many descriptions of Orkney and Shetland.

Below *Vinquoy, Eday.* Bottom *Benstonhall*

Chambered Cairn,
Vinquoy Hill, before 2000 BC
A small communal tomb of the Maeshowe variety. The 2.5m high central chamber is roughly circular and corbells inwards towards the top. Recently restored. *Open to the public*

84 **Benstonhall**, early 20th century
An especially well-constructed group of buildings in red Eday sandstone including the remains of a small waterwheel, which formerly drove threshing machinery, and its lade along the side of its long barn range. An adjacent outbuilding has a hipped roof of sandstone slabs, an unusual form in Orkney.

Mill, 19th century
A small, two-storey grain mill which, powered by water from Mill Loch, served the entire island estate.

Kirk, 1858
The former U P church, featuring a traceried west window and a small belfry. The gallery is supported on timber posts with Ionic capitals and reached by stairs with twisted balusters. The original gaslight fittings survive and a heavily carved font contrasts with plainer woodwork.

WESTRAY (see p 70)
Westray is the most scenically varied of the North Isles. Its long irregular form begins in the west with spectacular cliffs at Noup Head and the distinctive trio of Knucker, Gallo and Fitty Hills. From here it stretches eastward and southward across lower lying and productive land, with fringes of dazzling white sand at Noltland Links in the north and the broad bays of Tuquoy and Tafts on the south-west. It has retained its indigenous population and hence its island character: the Orkney accent is still strong and almost universal.

The sheltered bay at **Pierowall** has long been an important harbour, although **Gill Pier**, c.1875, centre for the modern fishing fleet, actually stands some way out of the original village, which lay at the head of the bay where some 18th-century decaying houses remain; most of the remainder of the village dates from the 19th century.

Below *Fishing store, Pierowall.*
Bottom *Lady Kirk, Westray*

Burgher

Fishing Store, 1883
A well-proportioned pierhead building fronted by freestone arches. Fish were salted in the store and, in winter, hung on hooks to dry over movable braziers.

Trenabie House, 1881
Two-storeyed and rendered with a porch and dormered upper windows.

Lady Kirk, 13th century; altered 1674
Roofless and oblong with a wide semicircular chancel arch in red and yellow sandstone and a small rectangular belfry at the west end. *Open to the public*

Pierowall Hotel, early 19th century
An unusual two-storey house end on to the road with one end of its flagstone roof piended.

Burgher

RCAHMS

Noltland Castle, *c.*1560

The grim fortress of Gilbert Balfour, who was implicated in the murder of Cardinal Beaton and served on a French galley alongside John Knox as a result. Later he became Master of Mary Queen of Scots' household and was brother-in-law of Adam Bothwell, Bishop of Orkney, before being found guilty of treason in 1561. A Z-plan castle, with square towers and thick walls pierced by 71 gunloops. Inside, a massive barrel-vaulted room, originally divided lengthways. A broad winding stair with carved Roman newel post rises to a roofless great hall. *Open to the public: guidebook available*

Orkney Library

Top and Above *Noltland Castle*

Baptist Kirk, 1850

Low and harled with a small porch and part piended roof in grey local slate.

To the north of Pierowall, around **Rackwick**, stands a scatter of old flagstone-roofed crofts in a magnificent setting above the sandy beach and looking across to Noup. The remains of a neolithic village contemporary with Skara Brae lie under the **Links of Noltland**.

Noup Head

86 ### Noup Head Lighthouse, 1898,
David Stevenson

A brick built, white-painted tower warning of the dangers of nearby North Shoal share its cliff-top perch with one of Orkney's main seabird colonies.

Trenabie Meal Mills

A pair of mills that formerly served the Balfours' estate: that sited closest to the village

Burgher

Top *Broughton*. Middle *Brough*.
Above *Cleat*

**The first of the Stewarts of
Brough** was Edward, a natural son
of Robert, Earl of Orkney. His great-
grandson, Archibald, was involved in
the Jacobite Rising in 1745 with the
result that the original house of
Cleat was burned to the ground on
26 May 1746 by Hanoverian troops
led by Benjamin Moodie of Melsetter.
Stewart escaped, along with David
Balfour of Trenabie and several
other Jacobite lairds whose homes
and property suffered a similar fate,
after taking refuge in the
Gentlemen's Ha: a cave in the
Rapness Craigs.

dating from the 18th century, its three-storey
successor from the following century.

Broughton, 19th century
An L-shaped terrace of harled houses, their
backs turned to the sea, built to accommodate
workers on the Brough Estate.

Brough, early 19th century
Currently abandoned, but a well-preserved
example of a small Orkney mansion. Its local
slate roof, grey like its harling, is dressed with
swept valleys around a chimney gablet which
rises above the stair to the first floor and attic.
A trim two-storey stone **farmhouse** stands a
little way off. The extensive stone-built
steading ranges in an E-shape around two
courtyards. As part of the process of
agricultural improvement, the valley was
gridded into a series of 20-acre fields
surrounded by stone walls, giving it a uniquely
homogeneous appearance.

Cleat, 18th century
One of a group of North Isles' houses burned by
Hanoverian troops. It was rebuilt in two stages
incorporating a plain rendered three-bay house
to the rear with a taller and more elegant two-
storey wing somewhat clumsily tacked on in
front. The old flagstone roof, lost to an Orkney
gale, has been replaced by corrugated asbestos.

Three **churches** overlook the valley. At Brough
the **Sheepy Kirk**, 1823 now a ruin, was the
first United Presbyterian Church, It still has
doors at either end, arched windows in the
south wall and signs of later gallery. It was
replaced by the **New Kirk** in 1866, more
elaborate with stone walls and pointed
windows. The **Old Kirk** or parish church of
1845 is an oblong barn with a part piended roof
in big local slates. Its interior is bright and cool,
with blue- and yellow-painted woodwork and a
canopy over the pulpit topped by the dove of the
Holy Spirit.

Fribo, 19th century
A large squarish-rendered mansion with
piended roof and central chimneys, overlooking
a walled garden which contains the only
sizeable group of trees on the island.

87 **Cross Kirk**, Tuquoy
A 12th-century ruined chapel with a barrel-
vaulted chancel, arched door and lancet

window. The nave was expanded in the 17th century when it served as one of a number of parish churches. *Open to the public*

Old Westside Manse, 17th century
A plain three-bay house expanded by a hulking wing to its front: this once-extensive residence of the Westray minister is now fast decaying.

A variety of mills survive at **Rapness**, in the south of the island, including the derelict two-storey **Rackwick Mill**, with an overshot wheel and, at nearby **Clifton**, a conical-roofed horse-gang. At **Sangar** is a small windmill at the end of an abandoned croft, the remains of its mechanism carried on two stone pillars. A tapering stone pillar standing in a field at **Helzie** was the base of a substantial windmill, like that in North Ronaldsay.

Helzie House, 18th century; altered
The original single-storey house is said to have belonged to a retired sea captain who had it roofed like the deck of a ship complete with a wheel-house. Much of the character of the house has been lost in a recent renovation.

88 **Rusk Holm**
The tiny island of Rusk Holm is occupied by a windowless stone house, formerly inhabited by the kelp gatherers. Square brick-lined chimneys commemorate an unsuccessful experiment in industrialising the kelp-making process.

A **fort** built of beach stones, on the skerry to the south, affords protection to native seaweed-eating sheep at high tide. A tiny stone-built bothy on nearby **Wart Holm** was built to shelter shipwrecked seamen.

PAPA WESTRAY
This mostly green and fertile island rises to a low ridge running from Vest Ness in the south for just over 7km to Mull Head, reaching a height of 48m at North Hill.

89 **Knap of Howar**, *c.* 3900-2800 BC
A farmhouse with workshop; the oldest dwelling in north-west Europe. The house is the southern building and was divided into two rooms by a partition of upright flagstones and timber posts: the entrance has been constructed to take a wooden door and opens into a room with a low stone bench to the right and a doorway to the workshop on the left. The inner room, with central hearth and quernstone, was

Cross Kirk

Patrick Neill in 1806 related: *Capt Richan has erected several reverberatory furnaces after the plan of Colonel Fullerton's in Ayrshire, for drying and burning the great tangle of red ware during winter – both what is tossed ashore by storms, and what is cut by his tenants at ebb tide in moderate weather. The kelp manufactured in these furnaces is purer than the common kelp and sells for a proportionally higher price. The want of coals is a discouraging circumstance and will probably prevent the general employment of these furnaces in Orkney.*

Rusk Holm

Knap of Howar

the kitchen. The walls remain to a height of up to 1.6m and, at 10m by 5m, it forms a fairly spacious dwelling. *Open to the public*

Holland House, Papa Westray, 17th century
The original rectangular block with attic was probably built for a son of Earl Patrick Stewart's Chamberlain, Thomas Traill, who obtained title of the estate in 1636. There are lower wings to the west and north, a flat-roofed porch to the south and, to the east, a walled garden. The interior includes 17th-century panelling. The farm buildings include a 19th-century large **horse-gang** with conical flagstone roof, a circular **kiln** and, at a slight distance, a **windmill**, only the rubble base of which survives.

Watermill, Hookin, early 19th century
A single-storey mill sited practically on the beach, and driven by an undershot wheel.

Holland House

St Tredwell's Chapel
Dedicated to St Tredwell (or Triduana), who is said to have plucked out her eyes to protect her virtue. Only the outline of the tiny rectangular pilgrimage chapel is now visible, set atop the remains of a curving broch wall.

90 **St Boniface Kirk**, originally 12th century
A diminutive rectangular chapel that formerly contained a gallery, reached by an external stair beside its west door; now derelict.

St Boniface Kirk, Papa Westray

NORTH RONALDSAY
North Ronaldsay lies at the north-east extremity of the island group. Five and a half km long and rising to just 20m, the island presents a large number of old croft houses, typically roofed with flags, though in a less regular fashion than in other islands.

Sheep Dyke
Unique built feature of North Ronaldsay, 19km long and encircling the islands thereby excluding the unique seaweed-eating sheep from all cultivated land. Gaps in the structure reduce the risk of gale damage. The sheep are

Croft, N Ronaldsay

gathered together or *punded* four times a year. The complex of **punds** at Dennis Ness is the most important of the gathering points on the island and it was here that the sheep were gathered for slaughter on Christmas Eve and at Hogmanay.

91 **Beacon**, Dennis Head, 1789,
Thomas Smith & Ezekiel Walker
One of the first four lighthouses in Scotland and constructed in undressed local stone. It was erected by masons John White and James Sinclair for the Commissioners of Northern Lights at an estimated cost of £199 12s 6d. Its fixed light survived until 1809 when, with the

Sheep, N Ronaldsay

Above *Dennis Ness*. Below *Beacon, Dennis Ness*. Bottom *Lighthouse*

illumination of *Start Point*, the cast-iron lantern with its copper-sheathed cupola was replaced by the huge ashlar ball which had topped the Sanday beacon.

North Ronaldsay Lighthouse, 1852,
Alan Stevenson (see p 72)
Built in brick and, at 42.3m, Britain's tallest land-based lighthouse. William Kinghorn from Leith tendered to build it for £681 8s 7d. Stone was restricted to the base and the arched corbels of the external gallery. As at Graemsay, Grecian heads decorate the brass lamproom ventilators.

Pier, Bewan, *c.*1852
The first jetty on the island was built by William Kinghorn. Massive stone slabs are set slant on edge and held with iron bands. The flag-roofed store at its head was used for fish curing.

Old Kirk, 1812 and 1906
A harled and crowstepped Parliamentary Church, given a castellated tower in 1906 to house a bell presented by W H Traill. The plain and well-proportioned interior with end galleries contrasts with a massive and heavily decorated wooden pulpit, also donated by the Traills.

Mill, Hooking, early 19th century
A single-storey flag- and thatch-roofed watermill with arched doorways for cart access. The undershot wheel has gone, but the timber-pegged drive wheel is still in place and the flagstone-lined mill lade intact.

Holland House, 18th century
The original house may have been built for
James Traill, an Edinburgh lawyer who bought
the island in 1727. Additions have been made to
the south, 1873, and west, 1905. This latter
work includes a castellated tower which just
about holds the whole composition together.

Holland House

Windmill, Peckhole, late 18th century
The last working windmill in Scotland,
commemorated by a tapering circular rubble
base, it worked until 1908 when it was replaced
by its oil-powered neighbour.

Left *Windmill, Peckhole around the
turn of the century.* Below *Bird
observatory*

Standing Stone, Holland
A lone, lichened 5m-high stone, pierced by a
small hole at a height of about 2m and the
scene of New Year dancing up until the early
18th century. More prosaically, it has been used
as a navigation mark in conjunction with two
nearby stone-built pillars, one a conical beehive,
the other rectangular and pyramid-topped.

92 **North Ronaldsay Bird Observatory**, 1985,
Jacques & Adams
An energy-efficient house, roughly pyramidal in
form with an L-shaped conservatory and long
kitchen/dining area wrapped around the south
of a two-storey block of living accommodation.
An air-circulation system with heat exchanger
makes the most of passive solar gain from the
conservatory, while the 10kW wind generator
installed in 1988 contributes heat to a 2000-
litre hot-water store.

ACKNOWLEDGEMENTS AND BIBLIOGRAPHY

This book could not have been produced without the assistance and co-operation of many organisations and individuals to whom the author is greatly indebted. Firstly, thanks are due to the sponsors: Occidental UK Consortium, Orkney Islands Council and the Highlands & Islands Development Board. Thanks also to the following for their assistance in research and obtaining illustrations: at Orkney Islands Council, Laurie Sparrow and the Department of Building Services; the Planning Department; Alison Fraser, David Mackie and the Orkney Library; Bryce Wilson and Orkney Museums Service; John Windwick at St Magnus Cathedral; Historic Buildings & Monuments Scotland; The Royal Commission on the Ancient & Historical Monuments of Scotland; James Simpson and Simpson & Brown Architects; Northern Lighthouse Board; Architecture Library, Edinburgh College of Art; the staff at Occidental's Flotta Terminal; Revd Fraser Penney; Graeme Orr, and all those people, too numerous to mention individually, who welcomed and introduced the author to their homes and property. For particular assistance and kindness, thanks are due to the late Mr R G and Mrs E Bain, Mr I Heddle, Mrs Joy, Mr D Robertson, Mrs Scarth, Miss E Seatter, Mrs Thomas, Dr K Woodbridge and the Zawadski family. For their assistance with travel arrangements, thanks to John Grieve and the crew of the mv *Mariana*; Steve Mowat and the crew of the mv *Jessie Ellen* and the Flaws family on the mv *Eynhallow*. Alice Groundwater and Margaret Kemp deciphered the author's handwriting and typed the early drafts, while at the RIAS considerable assistance has been given by Margaret Wilson, Emma Crawford, Helen Nicholson, and Lena Smith. The text has benefited from the expert advice of Dr David Walker, Dr John Frew and David Jones, and Duncan McAra's editing, while Charles McKean's advice and assistance have been invaluable. Thanks to Dorothy Steedman for her design, patience and cheese toasties. Personal thanks are due to friends and employers at Edinburgh College of Art Students Union, the Stillman Eastwick-Field Partnership and Roland Wedgwood Associates for their assistance and forbearance; to Christine Souter, David Galbraith and Donald and Sonia Rae for encouraging the author to undertake the project and their subsequent interest in it; to George and Freda Burgher, without whose assistance in so many ways this book could never have been begun, let alone completed, and to Clare Hammond (for whom it was written) for her drawings.

BARRY, G, **History of the Orkney Islands**, 1805; BEN, Jo, **A Description of the Orcadian Islands**, 1829; BERRY & FIRTH (ed.), **The People of Orkney**, 1986; BRAND, **A Brief Description of Orkney**, 1701; 1988; CHILD, V G & CLARKE, D V, **Skara Brae**, 1983; CLOUSTON, J S, **The Orkney Townships** (in *Scottish Historical Review*), 1919; CLOUSTON J S, **Old Orkney Houses I, II, & III, The Evidence of Stone**, *Proceedings of the Orkney Antiquarian Society*); CLOUSTON, J S, **The Orkney Parishes**, 1927; FENTON, Alexander, **The Northern Isles**, Edinburgh, 1978; FENTON & WALKER, **The Architecture of Rural Scotland**, 1981; FEREDAY, R P, **Orkney Feuds and the '45**, 1980; FEREDAY, R P, **The Longhope Battery and Towers**, 1971; FIDDES, J & ROWAN A, **David Bryce**, 1976; FIRTH, John, **Reminiscences of an Orkney Parish**, reprinted 1974; GOODFELLOW, A, **Sanday Church History**, 1912; GORRIE, David, **Summers and Winters in Orkney**, London, 1868; GROAT, J S, **W R Lethaby and Melsetter House**, (unpublished essay), 1980; GROOME, F, **Ordnance Gazeteer of Scotland**, 1822; HAMILTON-BAILLIE, J R E, **Coast Defences in Orkney in Two World Wars**; HEDGES, John W, **Tomb of the Eagles**, 1984; HEWISON, W, **This Great Harbour, Scapa Flow**, 1985; HOSSACK, **Kirkwall in the Orkneys**, 1901; IRVINE, W, **Isle of Shapinsay**, 1977; LINKLATER, Eric, **Orkney and Shetland**, 1965; LOW, George, **A Tour through ... Orkney and Shetland ... 1774**, MACDONALD, J, **Churchill's Prisoners**, 1987; MacGIBBON, D & ROSS, T, **The Castellated and Domestic Architecture of Scotland**, 1887-92; McGREGOR, **Descriptive Notes on Orkney**, 1890; MACINTOSH, W R, **Glimpses of Kirkwall and its People in Olden Time**, 1887; MARWICK, E, **A Gallery of Famous Visitors to Orkney**; MILLER, Ronald, **Orkney**, 1976; MILLER, Ronald (ed), **Third Statistical Account**, 1985; MOONEY, John, **The Cathedral and Royal Burgh of Kirkwall**, 1947; MUIR, Edwin, **An Autobiography**, 1954; MUIR, Edwin, **Scottish Journey**; NAISMITH, **Buildings of the Scottish Countryside**, 1985; NEIL, Patrick, **A Tour Through Orkney and Shetland**, 1806; **New Statistical Account**, 1842; OIC Planning Department; **Orkney Heritage Series**; Orkney Museums, **For Those in Peril – Orkney Lifeboat History**, 1977; PALSSON, & EDWARDS, **Orkneyinga Saga, Harmondsworth**, 1981; PALSSON, HERMANN & EDWARDS, PAUL, **Magnus Saga**, 1987; POCOCKE, R, **Tour of Scotland**, 1760; POW CHAPEL PRESERVATION COMMITTEE, **Agriculture in Orkney**, 1874; RENDALL, E, **Lest We Forget**, 1989; ROYAL COMMISSION ON THE ANCIENT MONUMENTS FOR SCOTLAND; **12th Report; Orkney**, 1946; RITCHIE, Anna, **Orkney and Shetland**, 1985; RITCHIE, A & G, **Ancient Monuments in Orkney**, 1986; RUEBENS, G, **W R Lethaby**, 1986; SCOTT, M A, **Island Saga**; SCOTT, Walter, **Tour with the Commissioners of Northern Lights**; SCOTT, Walter, **The Pirate**; SIBBALD, R, **Description of Orkney**, 1711; SIMPSON, W D, **Bishops' Palace and Earls Palace**, 1977; SMITH, J, **Church in Orkney**, 1907; SPENCE, S, (ED), **Old Orkney Trades**, 1988; **Statistical Account of Scotland**, 1791-99; SUTHERLAND, D, **Against the Wind**, 1966; THOMPSON, William, PL, **A History of Orkney**, 1987; THOMPSON, PL, **The Little General and the Rousay Crofters**, 1981; THOMPSON, PL, **Kelp Making in Orkney**, 1983; TROUP, James and Eunson, Frank, **Stromness**, 1967; TROUP, R, **Orkney Through Strangers Eyes**, 1986; TUDOR, R, **The Orkneys and Shetland**, 1883; TULLOCH, P A, **A Window on North Ronaldsay**, 1974; WILSON, B, **Lighthouses of Orkney**, 1975.

B

Baikie, Arthur 21
Baikie family 13, 31
Baikie, J Malcolm 17, 27
Baikie, William 17
Balfour, David 81, 82, 83
Balfour, Gilbert 94-5
Balfour, John 22
Balfour, William 28
Ben, Jo 54, 79
Benson, W A S 76
Berstane House 28, 28
Binscarth House 57
Birsay 43-5
  Bridge 44
  Lighthouse 45
  St Magnus Church 44
  St Peter's Church 45
Boardhouse Mill 43, 43
Braebuster, Deerness 32, 32
Brand, John 44
Breck of Rendall 58
Breckness 40, 40
Breckness Battery 33
Brig o' Waithe 54, 54
Broch of Gurness 59, 59-60
Brodgar, Ring of 53
Brough of Birsay 45
Brown, Ford Maddox 76
Brown, George Mackay 34, 38
Bryce, David 11, 28, 81, 82, 83
Burgar Hill Wind Energy Site 60, 60
Burne-Jones, Edward 76
Burray 62
  Bu 62, 62
  Sands Motel 62, 62
  Storehouse 62

C

Cairns, W J & Partners 67
Caithness, Earl of 14
Caldale Airship Station 29, 29
Calder, Peter 21
Carmichael Smith, Maj James 73
Chambers, William 16
Chiochetti, Domenico (POW) 61-2
Clestrain, Hall of 54
Click Mill 46
Clouston, Edward 36
Clouston, Sir Robert Smith 46
Copinsay Lighthouse 32
Corrigal Farm Museum 47, 47
Covenanters' Memorial 32
Craigiefield House 28, 28
Crawford, Andrew 11
Crear McCartney 10
Cursiter, Stanley 9, 10, 38-9, 39, 42, 43
Cuween Hill Chambered Cairn 56

D

Deerness 31-2
Denison, R 18
Dewar, R G 15, 40

Dounby 46
Doyle, Charles 5
Dundee University 67
Dunnet, William 18
Dunsyre 47, 48

E

Earl's Palace, Birsay 44, 44
Earl's Palace, Kirkwall 10-11, 11
Eday 92-4
  Benstonhall 93
  Carrick House 92, 92-3
  Kirk 94
  Chambered Cairns 93
  Stone of Setter 93
Egilsay 85
  St Magnus Church 84, 85
Elliott, Marvin 23
Erskine, James 19
Eunson, Reynold 9
Evie 58-60
  School 59
Eynhallow 86
Eyrland, Mill of 54

F

Fairlie, Reginald 46, 56
Fea, James of Whitehall 87, 87
Fea, William 12
Finstown 57
Firth 56
Flotta 67-8
  Buchanan Battery 67, 67
  Coastal Defence Battery 68
  Oil Terminal 67-8, 67, 68
  Port War Signalling Station 67
Foveran 29
Fraser, Eliza 37
Fulzie, Gilbert 13

G

Gairsay 86-7
  Langskaill 86, 87
Gilbertson, M M 15, 20, 21, 23, 29, 59, 77
Gimson, Ernest 76
Gladstone, W E 29
Goodfellow, Revd Alexander 92
Gow, John 54, 92, 93
Graeme family 32
Graemeshall 33-4, 33
Graham, Alexander 36, 36
Graham, Bishop George 33, 34, 40, 41
Graham Thomson, Leslie (MacDougall) 89
Greenwall 33, 33
Groat family of Tankerness 30
Groome, Francis 74
Gyre 59

H

Haakon Haakonsson, King of Norway 11, 63, 81
Harray 46, 46
Heriot-Watt University 67

Heron, Kate 36
Holland House, Harray 47
Holland House, N Ronaldsay 100-1
Holland House, Papa Westray 98
Holm 32-3
Holodyke, Harray 46
Honyman, Patrick 54
Hossack, Buckham Hugh 18, 23, 26, 28, 53
Houston, Thomas 26
Hoy 3, 68-80
  Bu of 78-9
  Burnmouth House 79, 79
  Burra House 78
  Dwarfie Stane 79, 79
  Graemsay 79-80
  High and Low Lighthouses 79-80, 80
  Longhope 74
  Lyness 77-8
  Martello Towers 74, 74
  Melsetter House 2, 75-7, 75, 76
  Rackwick 79, 79
  Rysa Lodge 78
  St Margaret & St Colm Church 76, 76
Hudson's Bay Company 37

J

Jack, George 76
Jacques & Adams 101
James III, King of Scotland 7
Jamieson, A T 17, 27, 36

K

Kemp, Marjorie 89
Kirbister Farm 45
Kirbister Meal Mill 56
Kirkwall 6-28
  Albert Hotel 17
  Albert St 15, 15-16, 16, 17
  Alton House 25
  Andersquoy 23, 23
  Ayre Hotel 19, 19
  Ayre Mills 20, 20
  Balfour Hospital 23
  Baptist Church 22
  Berstane Rd 25
  Bignold Park Pavilion 27, 28
  Bishop's Palace 11-12
  Bridge St 17-18
  Broad St 12, 14, 15, 16
  Castle 14
  Castleyards 15
  Clay Loan 22
  Cromwell Rd 24
  Custom House 16
  Daisybank 24
  Dundas Crescent 27
  Earl's Palace 10-11, 11
  East Church of Scotland 19-20
  East (Paterson) Church 26
  Folly 18
  Girnel 18-19
  Glaitness Primary School 20-1
  Gospel Hall 22

Grain Earth House 20
Grammar School 26
Great Western Rd 20
Gunn's Close 21, 22
Harbour 18, 19
Hatson Airfield 20
High St 23
Highland Park Distillery 28, 28
Junction Rd 20
Kirk Green 12, 13
Kirkwall Hotel 18
Klosses 6, 8
Laing Brae 27, 27
Laing Street 17
Library 16
Main St 22-3, 23
Malcolm Gilbertson Centre 23
Market Cross 12
Masonic Hall 14
Mounthoolie Lane 17
Old Tolbooth 13, 62
Orkney Islands Council Offices 25-6
Our Lady's Church 23
Papdale House 25
Papdale Mill 26
Papdale Primary School 27, 27
Palace Rd 12
Park Cottage 25
Post Office 20, 20
St Magnus Cathedral 7,8-10, 8, 9, 10
Sheriff Court 11
Ship Inn 18
Shore St 24, 24
Spence's Square 22, 22
St Catherine's Place 24, 24
St Olaf Episcopal Church 27, 27
St Olaf's Kirk 17
Strynd 15
Tankerness House 13
Town Hall 14
Victoria St 21-2
Walls' Close 21
Wellington St 23
West End Hotel 23, 23
Willowburn Rd 26
Kitchener Memorial, Marwick Head 43

L

Laing, Malcolm 15, 25, 25
Laing, Samuel 25
Langalour 57-8
Lee, J 40
Lethaby, W R 75, 76, 76, 77, 78
Levitt Bernstein Associates 36
Lindsay, Ian G & Partners 13
Linklater, Eric 46
Low, George 7

M

MacDonald, G 21
Mackay, Robert 21
Maeshowe 48, 48
Mainland 6-62

Margaret, Maid of Norway 63
Matheson, Robert 5, 11
Maxwell Davies, Sir Peter 79
Middlemore, Thomas 75
Millar, John D 18
Millquoy Meal Mill 657
Mirkady Fishing Station 32
Moira & Moira 23, 67
Moodie, Capt James 12
Morris & Co 76
Morris, May 75
Morrison, Andrew 15
Mossetter 58
Mowat, Margaret 21
Muir, Edwin 86

N

Neill, Patrick 91, 97
Ness Battery 39-40
Norse Earls 3, 6, 8, 44, 55, 73, 85, 86
North Isles 80
North Ronaldsay 99-101
    Bewan Pier 100
    Bird Observatory 101
    Dennis Head Beacon 99-100
    Holland House 101, 101
    Lighthouse 100
    Old Kirk 100
    Peckhole Windmill 101
    Sheep Dyke 99
    Standing Stone 101
North Walls 74, 77
    Garrison Theatre 77, 77
    School 77

O

Oglaby 40, 40
Orkney Islands Council 12, 15, 20-1, 22, 23, 45, 47, 59, 64, 77, 79
Orkney Producers Ltd 20
Orkneyinga Saga 6, 9, 34, 86, 86
Orphir 54-56
    Church 55
    St Nicholas Church 54-5

P

Papa Stronsay 88
Papa Westray 97-9
    Holland House 98, 98
    Hookin Watermill 98
    Knap of Howar 97-8, 98
    St Boniface 99, 99
    St Tredwell 99
Peace, Thomas Smith 5,12, 14, 18,19, 22, 23, 25, 26, 37-8
Platt, Thomas 20
Pococke, Bishop 12
Point of Ness 39

Q

Quildon Cottage 40
Quoyloo Church 42-3

R

Rae, John 54
Rango, Mill of 40, 40-1

Reid, Bishop Robert 10, 11, 26
Rendall 58, 58
Rennibister Earth House 56
Rhind, David 17
Richan, Capt William 22
Riddoch, John 14
Ring of Brodgar 53
Robertson & Hendry 38
Ross, Alexander 27
Ross, John 11
Rousay 83-5
    Blackhammer Cairn 83, 83
    Hullion 84, 84
    Knowe of Yarsoe 83-4
    Midhowe Broch 84, 85
    Midhowe Tomb 84
    Mill 85
    St Mary's Church 84
    Taversoe Tuick 83
    Trumland House 83, 83
    Westness House 84, 84
    Wirk 84
Rusk Holm 97, 97

S

St Andrews 29-30
St Clair, Henry, Earl 14
St Mary's, Holm 33
St Ola 28
Sanday 90-2, 90, 91
    Geramount 91-2, 91, 92
    Kettletoft 90
    Ortie 90, 90
    Scar 90-1, 91
    Start Point Lighthouse 91, 91
    Stove 90, 90
    Tresness 91
    Warsetter Doocot 90, 90
Sandwick 40
Scapa Flow 60-2
    Churchill Barriers 61, 61
    Harbour Building 29, 29
    Italian Chapel 61-2, 61
Scott, Sir Walter 18, 36 ,53, 54, 73, 74, 78, 79,80
Scott, Revd William 22
Scuan Bridge 47
Shapinsay 80-3
    Balfour Castle 81, 81
    Balfour Village 81-2
    Dishan Tower 81, 81
    Elwick Bank 82
    Lady Kirk 83
    Mill 82
    Sound Gateway 81, 93
Sinclair, James 99
Skaill:
    House 41, 41
    St Ninian's Church 32
    St Peter's Church 42
Skara Brae 41-2
Smith, Thomas 99
Smoogro House 56
South Ronaldsay 62-6
    Back Rd 64
    Balfour Battery 65, 65
    Cromarty Square 64
    Front Rd 64
    Herston 65
    Iron Age House 66
    Kirkhouse Meal Mill 66
    Lairdene 64, 64

Pentland Skerries Lighthouse 66
Pier 64
Quindry House 64
Roeberry 64-5, 65
Smiddybanks Gateway 64
St Margaret's Hope 63-4, 64
St Margaret's House 64, 64
St Mary's Church 66, 66
St Peter's Church 63
Swanson House 64, 64
Tomb of the Eagles 66
Tomison's Academy 65-6, 66
South Walls 68-73
    Cantick Head Lighthouse 73, 73
    Hackness Battery 73-4
    Osmundwall Churchyard 73
Sparrow, L E 17, 21, 23, 64
Speakman, Peter 64
Spence, J 46
Stenness 48, 53
Stevenson, Alan 79, 100
Stevenson, David 73, 95
Stevenson, Robert 70,91
Stevenson, Robert Louis 10, 11, 13
Stevenson, Thomas 73, 89
Stewart Earls 11, 17, 44
Stewart family of Brough 19
Stewart, Helen 21
Stewart, Sir James of Burray 12, 62
Stones of Stenness 53, 53
Strange, Sir Robert 21
Stromness 34-40
    Academy 40
    Community Centre 36
    Dundas St 37, 37
    Franklin Rd 37
    Graham Place 36-7, 37
    Haven 38
    Hellihole Rd 37
    John St 35-6
    Khyber Pass 37
    Leslie's Close 37
    Lighthouse Shore Station 38
    Melvin Place 37, 37
    Millar's House 35
    Museum 37
    Ness Rd 38-9
    Pier Arts Centre 36, 36
    Pierhead 35
    Primary School 36
    Puffer's Close 37
    St Mary's Church 36
    South End 35
    Speeding's 35-6
    Stenigar 38-9
    Stromness Hotel 35
    Town House & Masonic Hall 5, 35
    Warehouse 35
    White House 38
Stronsay 87-90
    Auskerry Lighthouse 90
    Huip 88
    Kildinguie Well 89
    Mill 89
    Moncur Memorial Church 89

Mount Pleasant 89
Rothiesholm School 89
Water Pumping Station 89
Whitehall 86, 87-8, 88
Sule Skerry Lighthouse 45
Sutherland, Douglas 89
Swanbister House 55-6

T

Tankerness 30-1
    Battery 30, 30
    Fishing Station 3, 31, 31
    Hall of 30-1, 30, 31
    Meal Mill 31
    North Church 31
    Old Manse 31
Tennyson, Alfred, Lord 26
Thorfinn the Mighty 42
Tormiston Mill 48, 48
Traill, John 21
Traill family of Holland 19
Twatt:
    Airfield 43, 43
    Kirk 43

U

Unstan Cairn 54

V

Viking Asmundsvagr 73

W

Walker, Ezekiel 99
Walls 68
Walls, James 20
Watson, George Mackie 10
Webb, Philip 76
West Aith 41, 41
Westray 94-7
    Baptist Church 95
    Brough 96
    Broughton 96
    Cleat 96, 96
    Cross Kirk 96-7, 97
    Fishing Store 94
    Fribo 96
    Helzie House 97
    Lady Kirk 94, 94
    New Kirk 96
    Noltland Castle 94-5, 95
    Noup Head Lighthouse 95
    Old Kirk 96
    Pierowall 94
    Pierowall Hotel 95
    Rapness Mills 97
    Sheepy Kirk 96
    Trenabie House 94
    Trenabie Meal Mills 95-6
Whall, Christopher 76
Whitaker, Sir Arthur 65
White, John 99
Wideford Hill Cairn 29, 29
William IV, King 15
Winksetter 47-8, 48
Woodwick House, Evie 58-9, 59
Wright, James 7, 34
Wyre 85-6
    Cubbie Roo's Castle 86, 86
    St Mary's Church 86